# PRAISE FOR *THE PARIS PARADOX*

"I had every intention of skimming through this book, hunting for quick business takeaways. But after the first page I literally slowed down and savored Shemin's beautifully written prose, enjoying a taste of the French life—every bit as productive, yet so much more meaningful and enjoyable. Thank you, Shemin, for showing all of us how to take a beat while still being our best selves at home and at work."

**—Lance Rosenzweig**
*CEO, Pitney Bowes*

"In an age of endless hustle, Shemin offers a refreshing perspective—blending the French art of living with the American dream. Through stories backed by experience and data, she proves that mastery at work demands a certain richness in life. As businesses chase innovation, *The Paris Paradox* shows that creativity isn't found in the glow of midnight screens but in the warmth of long lunches, vacations, and genuine human connections. A vital truth for our times—to lead better, we must first live better."

**—Pari Natarajan**
*CEO, Zinnov*

"With *The Paris Paradox*, Shemin offers great insights and valuable strategies around lifestyle and mindset changes that will truly upgrade and change your life for the better. Her wise insights offer an essential and heartfelt guide to understanding and implementing changes to truly live life to the fullest.

I am sincerely grateful for Shemin kindly sharing perspectives around life–work balance and having it all. A must-read!"

**—Larry Long Jr.**
*Founder and CEO, LLJR Enterprises, and Author of* JOLT!

"For years, I envied my European colleagues' work–life balance. Shemin delivers a step-by-step guide to making it a reality in America—practical, actionable, and long overdue."

**—Maria Weaver**
*Former Global President, Warner Music*

"Shemin Nurmohamed skillfully blends a results-driven approach with a genuine passion for leadership, crafting a compelling strategy that emphasizes authenticity and understanding of the executive landscape. This insightful and engaging perspective strikes a perfect balance, offering practical advice on how to achieve personal and team success."

**—Laura Schwinn**
*Independent Director and Executive Advisor*

"Nurmohamed gives us a road map for life–work balance that applies to thousands. Bring a pencil when you open this book. You will want to make sure you highlight its lessons."

**—Ana Chadwick**

*CFO, Insulet, and World Traveler*

"Kudos to Shemin for breaking down what once felt impossible—achieving real work–life (or life–work) balance. A must read for anyone craving more freedom and fulfillment."

**—Silvano Sansoni**

"Shemin Nurmohamed has managed to capture the timeless wisdom of the French into a road map that will materially improve your work and home life. A must-read book filled with life-changing insights!"

**—Rahim Hirji**

*Executive VP, Avallain*

"Shemin provides an eye-opening contrast between the working norms in France versus the United States and many other countries. These insights come with actionable suggestions for real changes in how to approach 'life–work' balance. Bring your highlighter—you will make a new to-do list that will lead to greater happiness for you and greater impact for your company or whatever type of organization you work in!"

**—Colleen Ostrowski**

*Senior Vice President, Visa*

# THE PARIS PARADOX

SHEMIN NURMOHAMED

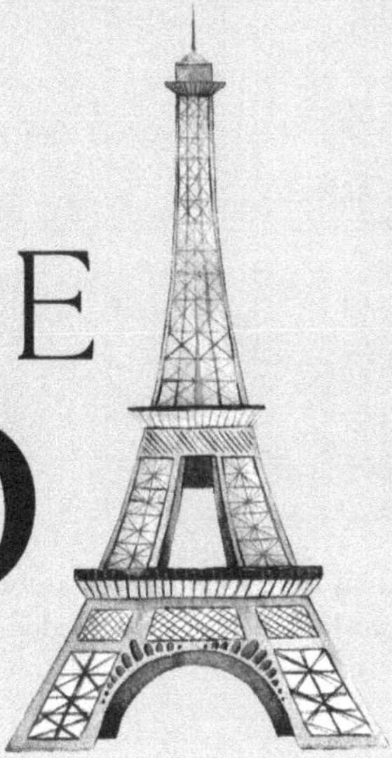

# THE PARIS PARADOX

## EMBRACING FRENCH IDEALS OF LEISURE TO TRANSFORM AMERICAN WORK-LIFE BALANCE

Forbes | Books

Published by Forbes Books, Charleston, South Carolina.
An imprint of Advantage Media Group.

Forbes Books is a registered trademark, and the Forbes Books colophon is a trademark of Forbes Media, LLC.

Printed in the United States of America.

10 9 8 7 6 5 4 3 2 1

ISBN: 979-8-88750-626-5 (Hardcover)
ISBN: 979-8-88750-627-2 (eBook)

Library of Congress Control Number: 2025908139

Cover design by Matthew Morse.
Layout design by Ruthie Wood.



05-30-2025 2:56

*To those who yearn for more—more joy, more contentment, more balance, more meaning.*

*To the dreamers with a little Paris in their souls, who embrace life's beauty with curiosity and passion.*

*To my husband, Fayyaz, and children, Qaahir and Aliya, whose unwavering support made every adventure possible—and yes, let this stand as the definitive word: The French experience was a great one.*

*And to the people of France, whose culture, spirit, and generosity have enriched my life immeasurably.*

# CONTENTS

INTRODUCTION . . . . . . . . . . . . . . . . . . . . . . 1

CHAPTER 1 . . . . . . . . . . . . . . . . . . . . . . 13
**The Art of Leisure**

CHAPTER 2 . . . . . . . . . . . . . . . . . . . . . . 27
**Changer d'air**

CHAPTER 3 . . . . . . . . . . . . . . . . . . . . . . 43
**Savor Every Meal**

CHAPTER 4 . . . . . . . . . . . . . . . . . . . . . . 57
**C'est la Vie**

CHAPTER 5 . . . . . . . . . . . . . . . . . . . . . . 71
**Cultivating Expertise**

CHAPTER 6 . . . . . . . . . . . . . . . . . . . . . . 87
**Le Village**

CHAPTER 7 .......................... 101
**Community and Connectivity**

CHAPTER 8 .......................... 119
**Conversation Authentique**

CHAPTER 9 .......................... 133
**Mastering Moderation**

CHAPTER 10 .......................... 151
**Cultivating Contentment**

CONCLUSION .......................... 167

THE PARIS PARADOX .......................... 171

ACKNOWLEDGMENTS, ET VOILÀ! ....... 173

ABOUT THE AUTHOR .......................... 175

# INTRODUCTION

I'd been at IBM's La Défense Paris office for almost three years. For all that time, despite enjoying my surroundings, I'd lived in an expat bubble at work. This was easy enough since my bosses were all American. Like them, I would grab a quick sandwich at lunch and get back to my desk as quickly as possible. Like them, I took fewer and shorter vacations than my French colleagues. Like them, I was always on call.

I'd started my career in the "strictly business" American style, and though it was demanding and uncomfortable, you could say it was my comfort zone.

My world began to change the day my friend Laura Miragoli pulled me aside. Laura was also an expat but of a very different sort. She was from Italy, and she'd blended into the French way of life instantly. The contrast between our lifestyles was immediately apparent. Although she worked in finance like me, she looked like she stepped right out of *Vogue*, with her Louboutin shoes with the red undersole and Hermes bag that perfectly matched her coiffed hair, makeup, and well-fitted suit. I had the slightly unkempt appearance of an overworked Canadian on my sixth cup of coffee for the day.

Ignoring the dark circles under my eyes—we had just closed the books on a particularly difficult quarter—she swept into my office, "Shemin, this is ridiculous. You have come to France. You are no longer American. You are French now. So, you are going to come with me and see how one should have lunch in a civilized country."

She dragged me downstairs to the IBM subsidized cafeteria while I tried to mentally tally just how long I could justify being away. I usually only took ten minutes to pick up a panini from a shop down the street. Stepping into the room, it was clear I'd need significantly longer. A French cafeteria is not like those you might have experienced in an American high school. There are similarly long tables, but the meal is three courses à la carte. When Laura and I arrived, there was a fifteen-minute queue just to find a seat. Checking my watch, I already felt like I was running behind.

But that's not to say I wasn't enticed by the experience. The cafeteria was a bustle of friendly conversation and laughter. In the air were warm smells of butter, shallots, and chocolate. I couldn't deny it felt like a pleasant diversion that far surpassed the mad race to the panini shop. Still, I had to get back.

I tried to make up some time by grabbing as few items as possible, but I was sandwiched between two people, and at each station, I was told I had to choose something. Appetizers, small main portions, cheese, a dessert: There was no escaping each choice. In the end, I chose salad vinaigrette, steak frites, and a macaroon.

Being used to how American meals played out, I fully expected that Laura and I would find seating where we could chat alone—or with a small group from finance. Instead, we sat down with a crowd, a mélange of people from across the entire IBM office. Feeling the minutes ticking away, I tried to salvage an excuse for not being at my desk by turning the conversation to business, but no one was willing to bite. Instead, everyone wanted to talk about life. One person across from me brought up their kids. Another farther down the table mentioned their recent vacation—they'd just returned from an active safari. Another still chatted on about their dog.

Business did come up from time to time, but it wasn't the focus. It was a natural extension of a conversation whose only purpose was finding and establishing a connection.

Eventually, that conversation turned back to me and work. Someone asked me what I did, and I shared my most recent business problem around international allocation strategies. My American bosses had spent four months on it, and they couldn't crack it. Saying this required a PhD to crack, they had handed it to me as if it was the most arcane and incomprehensible issue I'd ever face.

Instead of receiving sympathy and a sad shake of the head as I expected, one of the people listening immediately spoke up. "Oh, you should talk to Pierre. He works in treasury now, but originally, he created the allocation methodology. He knows all about that. Pierre!" They shouted at someone across the cafeteria. "Stop over here before you go."

When Pierre eventually sauntered over—with the slow, satisfied steps of someone well nourished by a good meal—he did indeed know the solution to my problem. I was stunned. In a single lunch, I'd found a solution for a quandary that had plagued my bosses for four months. I still had months left to solve it myself.

*Maybe there is something to these French lunches*, I thought. After all, Pierre was in a different department on a different floor. We shared no direct contacts that I knew of. I never would have even met him if I hadn't let Laura take me to lunch.

But it was time to get back. Lunch up to that point had taken an hour and ten minutes. Around me, the conversation was now accompanied by the clink of cutlery on recently emptied plates. With my business solution in hand, I sought an opportunity to make a run for it. But as soon as I tried to rise, a chorus called out. "Where are you going? *C'est l'heure du café.*"

Another twenty minutes passed over my *café allongé* (much to the disappointment of my colleagues, who strongly felt I should have ordered an espresso). My ten-minute lunch had turned into a full hour and a half. When I finally got back to my desk, I dreaded to think how far behind this adventure had left me. I already felt chronically behind. For months, I'd failed to complete each day's to-do list. No matter how hard I worked—no matter how few breaks I took—I couldn't check all the items off the list. How much worse would it be now that I'd lost ninety extra minutes of my day?

Yet when the day finished, I found, to my surprise, that I had actually done more than usual. I was so refreshed by my lunch, so invigorated by time away from thinking about business, that I'd come back with the energy and focus I'd been lacking.

For once, I'd put life first in the *life–work* balance, and it'd paid off twice. I'd solved an intractable problem, and I'd been more productive than I'd managed in months—and enjoyed a great meal!

As I left for the afternoon to return home to my family, I couldn't help thinking, *Maybe there* is *something to the French way of doing things.*

## The American Dream Versus the French Art of Living

Ninety-minute lunches spent building connections over great food—who wouldn't want to live that way? Back in America, it sounds like a dream in every sense. Not only is it ideal—it seems impossible. And it seems unfair. Why do the French get to take a whole month off, build strong communities, and live in beautiful, picturesque towns? How did America get it so wrong?

The roots of these differences are deep. In the early twentieth century, in his book *The Protestant Ethic and the Spirit of Capitalism*, Max Weber theorized that America is so work obsessed because of its religious origins. The country was founded by puritanical Protestants. One of their core beliefs was that God's favor is visible in how an individual acts in the world and how fortunate they are. A hard worker who earned more than others in their community was clearly among God's elect. And since being part of God's elect meant eternal salvation, that was quite a prized position to be in.

Alternatively, southern Europe remained Catholic, a belief system that saw devotion to God usually pull individuals away from worldly concerns and wealth. Compare the megachurch preacher of modern America to a Catholic monk, and you can see how different these ideas are.

Whether this is true or not is still debated—some argue the difference has to do with how northern Europe industrialized and modernized into the capitalist system. Either way, we now live in a world with two distinct views on work: We either live to work or we work to live. The American dream is built upon the former. We rise and grind. We stay late and work through weekends. We scale endlessly. We brag about how little sleep we need. Nothing is as important as success, and there's never enough success to challenge that assumption.

The French are undeniably capitalist in their economics, but they don't view their lives in this way. While the French way may be slower, it includes far more room for the things we really live for: time with friends and family, good food and good conversation, community, and moderation.

Increasingly, this is proving not just a preferable way to live but a necessary one. Our society is in the midst of a loneliness epidemic. Burnout is no longer a rarity in business; it's a constant threat. People are hurting from a lack of community and a life overwhelmed by work.

It doesn't have to be that way. The French prove it. I believe we can reverse these trends—one person, one family, one company at a time. After all, I'm living proof people can change. And what you may find, if you join me on this journey, is that your work can improve right along with your life.

## The Potential in Life–Work Balance

Reframing work–life into a life–work balance has many benefits. It offers us a chance to re-prioritize in a way that is more sustainable and pleasurable on a personal, communal, and even business level. On a personal level, these changes can improve your mental and physical health. Eating better, giving your body time to digest, taking time off, and building strong relationships—all of these have scientifically proven long-term benefits. As for family, these ideas can create the space to be as invested in your relationships as you've always wanted. After I adjusted to a life–work balance, I was able to drop off and pick up my kids every day. I had the time, energy, and focus to be present with them. They're now in their early twenties, but they still know they are my priority in their hearts and heads—because I was able to invest my time in them early, when their worldviews were forming.

On a broader level, these changes can build stronger, more active communities in which loneliness is a rarity. When I look at my kids, I see how few opportunities they have to connect in physical spaces.

That makes it very hard to develop the crucial social skills that we need to build friendships and work relationships. In a more balanced community, it's more common to pull someone into a conversation or a meeting. It's commonplace to bring someone coffee and engage in a chat. I'm confident we can rediscover these lost arts in America.

I know what you're thinking, *This all sounds great, Shemin, but what about the effects on business?* The truth is the French life–work approach actually *improves* your chances of success in business. For the individual, rebalancing your life can help you create a recession-proof skill set. By building connections, in the same way I did at that first lunch, for instance, you increase your knowledge and capabilities. While working in France, I ended up making several lateral moves in my career, giving me experience in sales, finance, product management, strategy, and pricing. I learned a great deal about other departments simply through osmosis over a good meal.

As AI is integrated into the workplace, employers will increasingly look for expertise not in a particular skill but in creativity and elasticity. It'll be about what you can learn and how you can connect ideas that will count. That's exactly what this approach offers.

And this isn't just useful on an individual level. France has long ranked as one of the most productive economies on the planet, not despite working in this way but because of it.[1] A workplace designed around a life–work focus is a happier environment for everyone. It increases cross-departmental understanding, builds a stronger culture, and creates loyalty. There's less turnover when people enjoy their workplace and feel it benefits the rest of their lives. Many workers will turn down higher pay for a workplace like that.

---

1 John Carney and Vincent Fernando, "French: The Most Productive People in the World," *Business Insider*, August 20, 2009, https://www.businessinsider.com/are-the-french-the-most-productive-people-in-the-world-2009-8.

In the words of Richard Branson, "If you take care of your employees, they will take care of the clients." That's particularly true in a country where these ideas are so uncommon. Making these changes can really help your company stand out.

The life–work French approach may even offer a solution to the remote work standoff we're seeing in many companies. Employees prefer remote work because they feel they lack the time to be with family and to live their lives. But work is less of a burden in France, where employees can expect long lunches, thirty-five-hour workweeks, five weeks off a year, and a strong communal experience in the office. Instead of struggling to see your spouse or your kids, you can be home for every dinner, have time every weekend, take long breaks to refresh yourself, and look forward to the strong relationships you've built in the office. If that were the deal on the table, how many more people would be willing to come back to the office?

## Too Good to Be True?

That's not to say there are no trade-offs when pursuing this realignment. In my own experience, I've found that the American approach to work will allow you to rise up the ranks faster. In making all those lateral moves in my career, it meant I moved up at a slower pace. I reached the top, but years after those who always put work before everything else.

There will always be people willing to work longer hours, give up weekends, and refuse to take vacations. Someone will always continue to skip lunch, and those individuals are likely to nab the next promotion.

In my opinion, though, this is an asset to the French way, not a deterrent. By rising more slowly, you're better equipped for what is ahead. You can learn more and cement your foundations so that when you eventually do reach the top, you'll truly be prepared for what the job requires.

Undeniably, though, this does mean you're more likely to earn less early on because you'll be trading money for time. Those workhorse colleagues of yours will beat you to the first opportunity for a bigger salary, allowing them to afford the new sports cars and bigger homes.

For those of you who prioritize those achievements over everything else, this book may not be for you. But if you'd rather have a healthy, happy, fulfilling life while you work, I feel this is a fair trade.

If you agree, you may have to find a different place to work. Culture is so important in attempting to implement these ideas—whether individually or top-down. There are companies out there that penalize workers for taking all their vacation time. Some businesses would rather let you go than allow you to take a longer lunch. These ideas won't work in those environments.

This is actually why I've landed at Pitney Bowes. The company has a long legacy of putting its people first. In the early days of the twentieth century, the leadership at the company would hire immigrants and encourage them to take paid classes to help them learn English. They hired African American people and women and had them work side by side for decades before that was the norm. They held town halls to get a sense of the issues bothering workers. To this day, the company invests in the education of its employees and their families.

It's the sort of environment where you can really live these values and implement them for others. Not every employer is like that. If you really want to incorporate these ideas, you'll need to find a partner in your employer.

Finally, it's important to recognize that this is not necessarily an "easier" way to organize your life and work. You have to invest the time to take the time. This means hard work, hitting deadlines, and proving your value to your employer. It means taking the time to train, invest in curiosity, build networks, and get things done. Remember, the French are not less productive than Americans—they actually get the same amount done in less time. If you want all the benefits, you have to commit to doing the same.

## Your Table Is Ready

It took me years to really embrace the French approach to life and work. I started going to lunches in the cafeteria after that initial experience, but it was another six years before I started taking all of my vacation—and it was legally mandated that I do so. In fact, I only started taking it because my file was audited. HR came to ask whether I was being abused by my American bosses.

"Do you know, Shemin," the HR representative said, "that you are even due extra holiday? As a mother and a woman over thirty-five, you are entitled to six full weeks a year."

I had been taking two.

Reluctantly, I scheduled a few weeks off. When I came back completely refreshed, full of disruptive new ideas, and actually excited to return to work, that's when I truly became a full convert.

Moving back to America years later, I discovered it wouldn't be so easy to bring the French way with me. No one was going to demand I take all my vacation. No one was going to suggest a long lunch. We've grown accustomed to weak social bonds in the office and in our communities.

That is the central paradox of this book: How do you create that French life–work balance in a country that doesn't even consider it a possibility? How can you remain successful and competitive—as an individual and a company—while implementing these ideas? How can you still grow in this environment?

Solving this paradox requires solutions that look a little different from how it's done in Paris. It involves different compromises, insightful leadership, and creative adjustments. You might not be able to take that mandated three consecutive weeks between May and September, but you may be able to negotiate an extra week on top of the two you already have. You might not be able to live in a beautiful, walkable city, but you can find a town with a nice little downtown area and buy a house within walking distance.

Whether you're an entrepreneur, a specialist, an executive, someone looking to retire who is perhaps nervous about how they'll spend their time once they are free of work obligations, or a leader looking to improve the life–work balance for the people you're responsible for, you have proven value that you can leverage. Use it.

To do this, though, it is much easier for those in a certain position. However, I believe these ideas are as valuable to a wage worker at McDonald's as they are for executives at Fortune 500 companies, but the former don't have the power or control over their time that the latter do. While some of you on an hourly wage may find it a bit more difficult to implement these concepts, there is still real value for you. I believe that anyone who has the talent, skills, and experience to demand more for themselves can be successful in this endeavor.

For those with the ability and motivation to embrace the French *mode de vie*, there is a path forward—even in America.

# CHAPTER 1

## The Art of Leisure

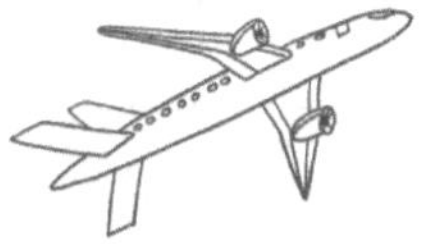

Fayyaz and I had been married for about a year. I was finishing my final assignment in London, England, for the company I was working for. Our next move was clear: We were packing up our home in Toronto and heading to Vancouver. When I got back, Fayyaz had packed everything already. Not only that—he handed me two tickets to Paris. *What a wonderful first-anniversary gift*, I thought. A second honeymoon in Paris before our big move. What could be more romantic?

But Fayyaz was distinctly unromantic on the flight. In fact, I noticed he was rather nervous. After some bumbling about and failing to make eye contact, he sprang his real surprise on me: We weren't visiting France; we were moving there.

Even worse than the "surprise," Fayyaz had already signed a contract, one that he didn't fully understand because he didn't speak French. I did, and as I was reading through the various clauses, I soon discovered that my husband's new company expected me to give up working. You can imagine how the rest of that flight went.

After the appropriate amount of time feeling sorry for myself, I was determined to make the most of this experience. After all, we'd be living in France. It was sure to be an adventure. We were settling in Chantilly, a pleasant small town just north of Paris with pre-Revolutionary charm—filled as it was with the elegant Château de Chantilly and its equestrian history. Within walking distance of our apartment, we'd have tree-lined canals and boulangerie carved into medieval buildings.

Despite what my husband's contract said, I was determined to work. Over the next few weeks, while Fayyaz jetted off on assignment to Tajikistan, I went to every financial institution I could and submitted my résumé. Dressed in heels and my best business outfits, I went door to door. In total, I visited more than three hundred locations. But the whole thing was useless. Once those in the office had finished laughing, each explained in turn that without a work visa or a degree in finance, they couldn't hire me.

I was puzzled by these encounters. It wasn't the laughter or the exasperating red tape—I understood that. It was how empty all the offices were. It was the middle of the summer, and most institutions seemed to barely be running. What was going on?

Hitting a brick wall on employment, I focused on getting everything we needed for our new apartment. If I couldn't find a job, I figured I might as well make us as comfortable as possible. Yet when I visited the shops, they weren't just half empty; they were closed. On one door after another, I found signs that read, *"Fermé pour les vacances 31 July to 24 Aug. Bonnes Vacances!" "Fermeture Annuelle," or "Congés d'été."* Each establishment was shut—not for a day but for weeks. The same was true for the bakeries.

I'd never felt so out of place. Clearly, I was missing something. How did these small businesses survive when they shut down for a whole month of the year? Surely, they were all setting themselves up to go out of business.

Giving up once again, I decided I'd simply spend my time enjoying my new country. I'd play tourist for a while. So long, sleepy Chantilly; I was off to gay Paris. Even in Paris, though, I found that half the cafés were closed. Those that were open had strictly prescribed hours with long breaks between lunch and dinner. Shops on every street were shut with the same now-familiar signs hanging in the windows. The City of Light, famous for its busy boulevards, was as empty of Parisians as the financial institutions. Most of the people who filled the streets were speaking English and other foreign languages—tourists just like me.

Still, it was hard to remain too upset as I explored those ancient cobblestone streets, taking in the elegant Haussmannian architecture against the blue summer sky. Eventually, I found a place that was open. As I sipped on an Americano—Europe's concession to American coffee preferences—I mulled over my experience of the last few days. I'd never seen a country with an advanced economy go on vacation. I'd arrived in France expecting adventure and leisure, but I'd clearly come at the wrong time of year for it.

## How the French Vacation

Before going any further, I feel it's important to say that my wonderful husband, Fayyaz, is, in fact, wonderful. I would eventually get all our furniture and find work—first as a chemistry teacher and then at IBM. In truth, I'm deeply grateful for Fayyaz's surprise now. France did turn into an adventure—one I'd never want to skip.

Back in those first weeks, though, I felt deeply out of place. It was Jean, the patron at the café where I sipped my Americano, who eventually demystified me. The French, he explained, have long taken all of August off. Their adherence to the annual *grandes vacances* amounts to a nationwide pause that offers everybody a chance to recharge their batteries. It's hard to imagine a stronger statement of priority of life over work than that.

The tradition, though, was born out of workplace necessity. As Jean related it, in the late nineteenth and early twentieth centuries, a huge number of people were employed in factories that needed a full production line of workers available at all times to run efficiently. If a factory were missing a key link (which was inevitable with staggered staff holidays), it would grind to a halt. As the demand for vacation time continued to rise, the government decided that the August holiday should be mandated to avoid unpredictable productivity dips at other times of the year. After all, that was also the time when schools were closed. If others were already getting a break, why not have everyone take it all at once?

These days, the policy has evolved somewhat, now guaranteeing three consecutive weeks off to every employee between May and September. August is still the most common month to take that time, though, particularly for those with kids.

This habit of taking vacation at the same time makes particular sense when you compare it to the American model, in which vacation is staggered. As the French predicted, this means we're often either missing a crucial member of the team or else there's pressure to keep vacations as short as possible. With everyone back in the office waiting for you to finish a particular task, it's hard to get away at all—and "getting away" often means working a little less while sitting on a beach.

This environment leads to some very dispiriting statistics. According to Forbes, 31 percent of workers have no paid time off (PTO) at all. Of those who do get PTO, the average number of days comes to a paltry eleven, while 52 percent continue doing some work during the days they do take off. In total, Forbes calculates that Americans waste an astounding *765 million vacation* days every year.[2]

I was part of the same trend. Even after embracing the French style of long lunches, I continued to take two weeks off or fewer each year for another three years. While my colleagues excitedly chatted about their plans for extended breaks a year ahead of the actual vacation, I kept to the American system: short breaks and last-minute planning. I didn't take my first three-week August break until HR confronted me during an internal/external audit and asked if I was being abused by my bosses.

Yet, just like those lunches, once I finally took the time off, I realized how much I needed it. And now, I cannot go back!

## The Value of a Good Break

I'm convinced everyone would love a month away from work. No matter how much you like what you do, no matter how much satisfaction the work gives you, if you could have a few weeks to relax, would you really refuse to take it?

The draw of a long break isn't laziness; it's the wisdom of your own body and mind. There's voluminous research that shows the value of an extended vacation. Working for long stretches without a break can affect how well we think. It can lead to "cognitive fatigue, difficulty

2 Anna Baluch, "Average PTO in the US and Other PTO Statistics," *Forbes*, March 30, 2023, https://www.forbes.com/advisor/business/pto-statistics/.

concentrating, forgetfulness, and impaired problem-solving ability."[3] Continuous work also wears down our bodies, raising our levels of stress hormones such as cortisol and epinephrine. This weakens our immune system, ironically making it more likely we have to call in sick.[4] A UK study that measured blood pressure, sleep quality, and resilience to stress found that they improved by 6 percent, 17 percent, and 29 percent, respectively, simply by taking a holiday.[5] It can also lead to long-term health issues. One study that tracked 749 women found that those who took vacations twice a year were six times less likely to develop heart problems than those who went six years or more without a break.[6] A study of more than a thousand middle-aged men found that those who took fewer than three weeks of vacation had a 37 percent chance of dying earlier.[7]

To avoid these health risks, any vacation is better than no vacation—but that doesn't mean that all vacations are created equal. A study by Finnish researchers found that subjects reached peak holiday happiness on day eight of their breaks.[8] This matches the French

---

3 Rebecca Zucker, "How Taking a Vacation Improves Your Well-Being," *Harvard Business Review*, July 19, 2023, https://hbr.org/2023/07/how-taking-a-vacation-improves-your-well-being.

4 Ibid.

5 Adrian Bridge, "Holidays Are Good for You—It's Official," *The Telegraph*, January 31, 2013, https://www.telegraph.co.uk/travel/news/Holidays-are-good-for-you-its-official/.

6 Elaine D. Eaker et al., "Myocardial Infarction and Coronary Death Among Women: Psychosocial Predictors from a 20-Year Follow-Up of Women in the Framingham Study," *American Journal of Epidemiology* 135, no. 8 (April 15, 1992): 854–864, https://doi.org/10.1093/oxfordjournals.aje.a116381.

7 European Society of Cardiology, "Take a Vacation—It Could Prolong Your Life," *EurekAlert!*, August 28, 2018, https://www.eurekalert.org/news-releases/490528.

8 Jessica de Bloom et al., "Vacation (After-) Effects on Employee Health and Well-Being, and the Role of Vacation Activities, Experiences, and Sleep," *Journal of Happiness Studies* 14 (May 12, 2012): 613–33, https://doi.org/10.1007/s10902-012-9345-3.

experience. As it was explained to me, it takes almost a week for your body to truly let go of work stress so it can truly relax. If that's all you're taking, then by the time you're ready to rest, you're heading back to work. If you add a second week, you actually give yourself the chance to recuperate. If you've never taken two weeks off in a row, let me tell you, that second week is true bliss. And if you're lucky enough to be able to add a third week, then you can spend it slowly preparing yourself to return to work. By the time you're back, you'll feel like you're ready to jump in and get back to it. And frankly, you'll be excited to do it.

The French subscribe to this framing so much they have a special word to describe that September back-to-work feeling: *la rentrée*. Once again, there's science to back the French up on this sentiment. One study found that for every ten additional hours a worker took, their productivity rose 8 percent.[9] Another study found similar improvements among high-level workers who had mandatory vacation time away.[10]

Less stressed, more focused and energetic—and more eager to work—a good, long vacation can do wonders for individuals and companies. It seems a bit of leisure goes a long way to making us happier, healthier, better workers.

## Taking a Break in America

If you're working in France right now, all of these points are common sense to you. But if you're in America, it's likely this all feels like an unachievable dream. Who gets a month off in America?

---

9 Lolly Daskal, "4 Scientific Reasons Vacations Are Good for Your Health," *Inc.*, June 13, 2016, https://www.inc.com/lolly-daskal/4-scientific-reasons-why-vacation-is-awesome-for-you.html.

10 Ibid.

In truth, there are some American companies that make it possible to take that kind of time off. Companies such as Adobe, LinkedIn, and Roku—among several others—offer one form or another of "unlimited vacation."[11] So long as you get all your work done on time, you're welcome to take as much time away as you want.

Unfortunately, this policy often has the opposite of its intended effect. Studies have found that workers tend to take less time off when offered unlimited vacation days, not more. The combination of "peer pressure and perceived expectations" leads workers to feel they should cut down on time off instead of maximizing it.[12]

I believe this policy often gets a bad name, though, because of the tech companies that often offer it and don't stand by it. In my experience, more traditional businesses tend to be more earnest in this policy.

This was certainly the impression I got from Siddhartha Mukherjee, an executive director at Warner Bros. Discovery (not the author, in case you were wondering, though they share the exact same name). He'd just come back from two-and-a-half weeks in Europe—and that wasn't the only vacation he was taking that year. When Siddhartha came to Warner Bros., he left a position that guaranteed him five weeks off each year, and he was determined to take those days in his new job.

Not only that, but Siddhartha pushes his team to take advantage of the policy as well. While I was speaking to him, he reminded a member of his team that she was going to be on vacation and not to commit to work during that period.

---

11 Jamela Adam, "20 Companies That Offer Unlimited Vacation Days," *U.S. News & World Report*, May 10, 2024, https://money.usnews.com/careers/slideshows/companies-that-offer-unlimited-vacation-days.

12 Bryan Lufkin, "The Smoke and Mirrors of Unlimited Paid Time Off," *BBC*, May 23, 2022, https://www.bbc.com/worklife/article/20220520-the-smoke-and-mirrors-of-unlimited-paid-time-off.

Taking that kind of time off in the summer is also possible at the small business level. We have an amazing French bakery in town called Raphaël's. It opened in 2020 and is run by a family of third-generation *boulangers/pâtissiers* from Brittany. Last August, Fayyaz and I went there to get one of their delicious baguettes for lunch, only to find the place shut for three weeks.

The next time it was open, I asked about this. They told me they always take August off—carrying on the tradition from France. What's more, they found they didn't lose any business at all. Despite this being the time of year when people crowd into town, their summer earnings didn't suffer. Instead, they were extra busy earlier in the summer and in September. People simply visited more often before and after the family's break.

For the rest of us, taking all of August off—or any other month for that matter—isn't even a theoretical possibility. That said, there are a number of ways you can improve the amount and quality of your leisure time.

First, you can start by taking all the vacation days that your company offers you. If you get ten days, take all ten each year. If you get fifteen, take them—and try to take two consecutive weeks off. One way to do this if you're stretched for days is to combine your time off with national holidays.

And if you work in a place that offers some version of unlimited PTO, try to take a month or even five weeks—even if your colleagues are cutting back.

There may also be opportunities to negotiate more vacation time. Many companies allow you to "buy" a week of vacation. For a reduction in your annual pay, you can add a week off to your year. You can even buy vacation at the start of a new job. The next time you're negotiating a new position, make it clear that you're coming partly for the time off. Set the parameters from the beginning. If your pay is already based on the time you'll take off, it's easier to guarantee you'll always have that time.

No matter how much time you get, though, be sure to make the most of it. You can start by truly taking a break. That means no communication from work and as little technology as possible.

Twenty years ago, nobody would take their computer on vacation. There was no expectation that you'd be available and willing to answer work questions on your time off. It isn't always possible to completely pull away from work, but where possible, a tech-free holiday should still be the ideal. In the States, senior executives are often expected to take work away with them, even if the "official" advice of their company says otherwise. Don't fall into that trend.

To free yourself of that responsibility and truly go offline, you have to prepare your team for your vacation. This starts with hiring well. You need people you can trust in place so you can delegate responsibility for an extended period. Your people should be comfortable—even excited—to carry on your work.

With those people in place, create a system that allows work to continue in your absence. Before I leave for a vacation, I lay out very clear instructions and guidance on all my projects. I explain what I've been working on and the steps to continue making progress. They know that when I come back, I'll expect notes on what they did and the decisions they made. That last point is key. You have to trust your colleagues to make decisions without consulting you. It takes a leap of faith the first time, but building up that trust improves your team and creates a culture of collaboration. It has the added benefit of developing next-level executives.

It also permits others to take time off. I always make my vacation time public because I want those around me to know that I see vacation as an asset, one that everyone should take advantage of. To make time off even more available, I pair people to be each other's backups. When one is on vacation, the other is there to cover. The only catch is they can't go on vacation at the same time.

Learning from my experience at IBM, I often check in with my team halfway through the year to see who has vacation time they haven't claimed. For those who haven't scheduled time away, I remind them that the company won't pay them more for working fifty-two weeks. That vacation is already figured into their salary, so they're essentially giving up two weeks' pay. Often, this slight nudge is enough to get them to set aside a week or two.

Once a team member is on vacation, I also model the behavior I want out of everyone. This means no communication unless there's an emergency. One member of my team, Gitika, had been working for the company for twelve years when she entered my department. When she told me she was going to India to visit family, I made it clear to her that she would not be hearing from me over the next three weeks.

Her family later told me that it was the first time in twelve years that her phone didn't ring the entire time she was home. She usually worked the same number of hours, just in a different time zone. This time, Gitika was able to actually relax and focus on being home. She knew that either Surya Sagi—our head of software engineering—or I would back her up so the work wouldn't pile up while she was away. Free of that concern, all she had to focus on was enjoying her time.

Before she left, she had been a real candidate for burnout. Hardworking, ambitious, and pivotal to so many of our big projects, she was clearly worn out. She came back better rested than ever before, and the speed at which she was promoted after she started taking these trips actually increased.

That's not to say more vacation always leads to faster promotion. In all honesty, I have to admit that sometimes it slows things down. Some companies will see a person taking their full allotment of vacation and will promote those who are in the office every day, no matter what. Other companies may even penalize those who take vacations. That may mean you have to find a better employer or accept a slower rise up the ladder. It's a trade-off. But when you return from two weeks of rest, I think you'll find it's worth it.

## Just Ask

Even in the best work environment, you can't just up and take a break whenever you want. At Pitney Bowes, we've recently had a change in CEO. If I'd had a vacation planned for the next month, I would have had to delay it. The French spend the summer getting their work in a place where they can step away for a month. The same is required in America. You have to put thought and strategy into the time you take off. You have to put the work in so you can take the time out.

It's June now, and I have to invest the time into getting to know the CEO's ideas and the strategy he wants to implement. But I'm still taking two consecutive weeks this year. That's far enough away that I can get my team on track to meet the CEO's targets for the first ninety days. I know my people will be capable of executing while I'm gone. In fact, my vacation will be a chance for them to shine.

Coming back to America, I have had to give up on taking the full month of August off, but I still get those two weeks in August (or in exceptional circumstances, at another time) and more time elsewhere in the year. I make sure I take a full month off out of every twelve. I secured that time when I came to Pitney Bowes by being upfront about my expectations. I learned long ago that one of the keys to getting more vacation is simply being willing to ask.

When my kids were still young, I was determined to do it all. I was going to be the mom of the year and the best executive at IBM, all in one. I was going to drop the kids off myself, work while they were at school, pick them up, spend quality time with them, cook dinner, put them to bed, and then get back to work.

That plan worked just fine for the first week. It was less fine the second week. By week four, I was staying up until two in the morning to complete the tasks I'd been assigned.

Then I got *the call.* I had missed an assignment. A junior manager in the global financial planning and analysis group was threatening to fire me. Trying to do everything without taking any breaks, I'd completely missed a piece of work. Not seeing any alternative, I quit. I couldn't keep this up, and I wasn't going to sacrifice that time with my kids.

After I sent an email with my resignation to my boss, he took a taxi out to our home in the middle of nowhere.

Seeing how exhausted I was, he said, "Shemin, I'm not accepting your resignation. Take two weeks off. We'll figure something out."

It was precisely what I needed. Two weeks, even just spent at home with the kids, helped me catch my breath and recover. During that break, I told my boss about the schedule I felt I could maintain. I could work from nine-thirty to three-thirty every day but Wednesday. I fully expected this to be declined, but I'd already quit anyway, so I thought I might as well take a chance.

A few days later, he told me there were three managers who could accommodate my new schedule. I went with Mike Newsam over the one that was better on paper because I knew Mike was a real family man. I was confident he would understand my new priorities.

My son later told me those were our family's best years together. And I'd only been able to secure our time together because I'd asked.

---

## *La Vie Française in America*

Three ways to start living the French lifestyle today

1. Plan your yearly vacation by January 5. Prioritize it and communicate it. This will give you ample time to find a backup, the best chance to buy tickets at a lower price, and set dates and a location to look forward to. Make sure all your days are accounted for so you take full advantage of your allotted time off.
2. Find a vacation buddy: someone who shares your passion for time away and can cover when you take your days off. Coordinate so you avoid any overlap in vacation dates. Also, make sure you both understand what constitutes an emergency and how to handle it. Then, share your buddy's info with your team so they know who's covering you. This will add an extra level of comfort for them when you're away.
3. Ask for one thing from work. It could be as small as an extra vacation day or as big as the freedom to work remotely for several weeks a year. Whatever will help you restore your energy. The worst thing your boss can say is no.

---

# CHAPTER 2

## Changer d'air

A French Sunday is a thing to behold. When I first arrived there, I couldn't believe how many businesses were shut. The usually boisterous streets were still. The outdoor tables at the cafés were unoccupied. Where the day before, you would have found neighborly chatter at the florists and busy hands testing the quality of fresh fruit in the market, doors were now shut, lights off, and stalls seemingly abandoned.

The roots of this tradition stretch back hundreds of years. Sunday had once been a holy day for almost everyone in France, as it was everywhere in Europe. Over the course of the nineteenth century—after the revolution and during the era of industrialization—French society temporarily reversed this practice. Factories didn't care for social customs, and most French people worked seven days a week. Everything was once again set right in 1906 when the Assemblée nationale passed a law severely curtailing labor on Sundays.[13] Even today, outside touristy areas such as the Latin Quarter and the first arrondissement, you'll find Paris is remarkably quiet.

This makes for very peaceful living for the locals, but it does present a problem for a mother trying to entertain two young children, a problem I was very much presented with after my son, Qaahir, was born. Now a family of three, Faayaz and I decided to move to the city. It was easier to find childcare there, and it cut down on my commute time. We moved to 8 Avenue Frémiet, into an apartment on the second floor of a Haussmannian building that the previous owner had decorated with high ceilings and gold-tinted moldings. Residing above a circular stairway, our two-bedroom apartment was perfect for a small family. There were only two apartments per floor, and we were steps away from the Seine. Just outside our front door, you could turn left to reach the river or turn right and find your way to the chic Passy neighborhood in the sixteenth arrondissement.

You might think that being situated in the center of Europe's second-largest city would offer plenty of opportunities for Sunday entertainment, but even in that location, I had trouble finding things to do to keep Qaahir busy. If we'd been back in America, we would have had access to unlimited entertainment options every day of the year, but in Paris, closed shops made for limited options. Eventually, I stumbled upon a solution in the form of a giant glass pyramid on the right bank of the Seine: the Louvre. The Louvre had multiple advantages for a young family. First, when everything else was closed, it was always open (except on Tuesdays). Almost as importantly, it was temperature controlled. In winter, it was warm; in summer, it was

13 Jeanine Cali, "How Sunday Came to Be Established as a Day of Rest in France," *Library of Congress*, September 2, 2014, https://blogs.loc.gov/law/2014/09/how-sunday-came-to-be-established-as-a-day-of-rest-in-france/.

cool. It's also big—with plenty of space to walk around and explore. Finally, it is home to more incredible art than you can imagine. If you've never been, take the largest museum you've ever visited and triple its size. That's the Louvre. In other words, for a curious young kid like Qaahir, there was always something new to discover.

Qaahir and I fell into a comfortable routine. Each Sunday morning, we'd have a nice, lazy lie-in before heading to one of the few open cafés in the area for breakfast—a croissant or *pain au chocolat*. We'd then make our way on foot through the largely empty streets to the museum. Back then, there was less security at the Louvre. If you were local and already had tickets, you could use a special entryway to skip the lines and head straight in. IBM graciously subsidized my tickets as part of the *comité d'entreprise* benefit so we could slip in right away with the other Parisians.

We usually arrived just before noon, right when the doors opened and before the crush of eager tourists became overwhelming for Qaahir. You might assume an enormous museum full of untouchable, unmoving objects would bore young children, but Qaahir took to it immediately. He came to love artists such as Leonardo da Vinci and Eugène Delacroix. Each Sunday afternoon, we'd choose three or four pieces to really take in. I'd read out what the plaques said and discuss what each painting or statue might mean.

Later, as he got older and his sister, Aliya, joined the routine, we changed things up a bit. By then, Van Gogh had become Qaahir's favorite artist, and since his work was only available across the Seine in the Musée d'Orsay, we often went there instead on Sundays. If we weren't in the mood to stare at paintings, we'd find other activities, such as going back to Chantilly to pick berries or going to the *marchés* in the region for the freshest food.

No matter where we went, though, we made sure Sundays remained special. They became our opportunity to experience what the French call *changer d'air*—a "change of the air" that comes from being in a different environment. The French believe that changing your outside environment can change your insights and perspective. That was certainly our experience. These outings replenished us, inspired us, and gave us a chance to make the most of our time together.

## Take a Day Off

For thousands of years, people have recognized the importance of taking a day off every week. For Jews, that day is Saturday, the Sabbath. For Christians, it's traditionally been Sunday. Islamic countries dedicate Friday and Saturday to prayer and rest. As in France, though, with industrialization, this tradition has eroded. Particularly in America, where we have weaker labor laws, work and other responsibilities have managed to crowd out our weekly time off. Not only do we fail to change the air, we end up doing the same things every day: work, sleep, work, sleep, work, sleep.

Modern technology has only exacerbated this trend. Business commitments sent via email, text, and social media encroach on us from every direction. We don't block time off. If we aren't working, we're "working" to prep for the week ahead—buying groceries, cleaning the house, paying the bills, and so on. Our "time off" is filled with errands that continue to deplete us as much as our work. At this point, some question whether we should even consider Saturday and Sunday a weekend at all.[14]

---

14 Katrina Onstad, "The Concept of the Weekend Is Dying," *NBC News*, November 3, 2017, https://www.nbcnews.com/think/opinion/concept-weekend-dying-ncna817131.

Working every day without a break is as bad for our physical and mental health as working without a proper vacation. The same health risks that we covered in the last chapter apply here, and there is similar value in taking these shorter moments of respite from work and other responsibilities. Using studies that have tested the effects of adding a third weekend day, we can extrapolate how important our days off are. The World Economy Forum has found, for instance, that an extra day off improves mental and physical health, as well as productivity.[15] Other studies back this up. Iceland has cut back on expected working hours each week from forty to thirty-five and has seen no loss of productivity. Meanwhile, a study in the UK piloted the four-day week, and afterward, 92 percent of the companies stuck with it—for obvious reasons. These companies had increases in revenue and improvements in health while seeing decreases in staff leaving, burnout, and stress.[16] If that's all true of a third day off, it's clear working on Saturday and/or Sunday can only have the opposite effect.

I don't want to focus on the time itself as much as what you do with it. After all, even in America, more than 70 percent of workers have the weekend off.[17] You have the time. The question is whether you're using it well.

Early in my career, when I worked at the hedge fund D.E. Shaw on Wall Street, I observed the "work hard, play hard" mentality that New York is famous for. The hours at work were long and grueling.

---

15 Douglas Broom, "Four-Day Work Week Trial in Spain Leads to Healthier Workers, Less Pollution," *World Economic Forum*, October 25, 2023, https://www.weforum.org/agenda/2023/10/surprising-benefits-four-day-week/.

16 "Prenups, Gen Z, and Iceland's Experiment," *The Female Quotient Newsletter*, November 26, 2024, https://newsletter.thefemalequotient.com/p/prenups-gen-z-icelands-experiment.

17 Niall McCarthy, "Americans Work Nights and Weekends the Most," *Statista*, October 10, 2014, https://www.statista.com/chart/2812/americans-work-nights-and-weekends-the-most/.

When everyone finally got away, they really let loose. Time off was almost as exhausting as time on. In essence, everyone was always "on." Everyone was working, or thinking about work, or playing hard enough they could finally forget about it for a few hours. No matter what, work dominated their lives.

In France, time off is meant to really involve time away from work concerns. It isn't a chance to catch up on email or get ahead on an assignment. In fact, it's very much meant to be the opposite. The French take the need for time away from work seriously enough that it's now illegal to email workers after normal business hours.[18] And this isn't just an exclusively French policy. Australia has also given workers the legal right to ignore communication from the office when they're off.[19]

But it isn't just a matter of avoiding work responsibilities. The French also wouldn't spend all their weekend getting around to dusting the apartment ahead of a busy week. Instead, they use that time to attend their children's school events, take up hobbies, and spend time with friends.

If you think of life like a pie, instead of work taking up almost the whole thing (as it does in America), in France, the other "slices" that give life most of its purpose—such as family, friends, new experiences, and outside interests—are much larger. This doesn't shrink the effectiveness of the work piece of the pie. In the end, the pie is simply larger.

18 Tod Perry, "Under French Law, Businesses Can't Email Employees After Work Hours," *Upworthy*, May 27, 2024, https://www.upworthy.com/under-french-law-businesses-cant-email-employees-after-work-hours-rp2.

19 Wing Kuang, "Australia Gives Workers Right to Ignore Bosses' After-Hours Calls, Emails," *Al Jazeera*, 26 August, 2024, https://www.aljazeera.com/economy/2024/8/26/australia-gives-workers-right-to-ignore-bosses-after-hours-calls-emails.

Americans used to have bigger pies as well, but a combination of longer working hours, social media, and crumbling social structures has left us facing a loneliness epidemic.[20] Our lonelier, emptier lives increase our risk of mental health issues such as depression and anxiety, as well as physical health risks, such as cardiovascular disease and diabetes.[21]

At the same time, freeing ourselves up to engage in leisure activities improves our ability to cope with stress.[22] It also improves our creative thinking. In our brains, there are two networks that act like bookends for our thinking. One, the control network, is responsible for logical thinking and analysis. The other, the default network, is responsible for mind wandering, creative, and lateral thinking. For the default network to work properly, relaxation is essential, as the stress hormones adrenaline and cortisol that result from working in a high-pressure environment trigger the control network. Daily practices such as meditation and exercise can help to restore the balance somewhat, but they are not enough to ensure the default network can flourish. To truly increase the prevalence of those elusive "aha" moments we're all chasing—the ones that lead us to those valuable new solutions to our old, intractable problems—we need to relax. That's why such moments so often occur when we're showering, walking, or playing tennis.

Albert Einstein believed he had most of his best ideas while riding his bicycle. The novelist Haruki Murakami once commented, "Most of what I know about writing I've learned through running

---

20 "Why Americans Are Lonelier and Its Effects on our Health," *PBS*, January 8, 2023, https://www.pbs.org/newshour/show/why-americans-are-lonelier-and-its-effects-on-our-health.

21 "The Epidemic of Loneliness," *eClinicalMedicine* 66, no. 102395 (2023), https://doi.org/10.1016/j.eclinm.2023.102395.

22 Yuta Takiguchi et al., "The Relationship Between Leisure Activities and Mental Health: The Impact of Resilience and COVID-19," *Applied Psychology: Health and Well-Being* 15, no. 1 (2022): 133–151, https://doi.org/10.1111/aphw.12394.

every day."[23] Composers Tchaikovsky, Beethoven, and Erik Satie all were avid walkers.[24] This is no coincidence. Original ideas often come about as a result of a combination of unlikely thoughts thrown together in a new way. They result from lateral leaps in thinking—the unusual knitting together of memories, insights, and thoughts that reside in the subconscious. You can't consciously think your way to an epiphany. Rather, you have to facilitate the conditions that are most likely to let one occur.

In other words, filling our free time with leisure activities is key to our ability to develop new, big ideas. "Work hard, play hard" leaves no room for this at all. Nor does it leave room for the value of novelty—or trying new things and meeting new people. In neuroscientific terms, novelty is recognized as one of the biggest positive factors for encouraging neuroplasticity—the growth of new pathways in the brain. When we experience new cultures, try out new hobbies, enjoy new foods, and meet new people, our brains carve out new pathways. This strengthens our ability to learn and remember.[25] It may also help our brains fight disorders such as Alzheimer's disease.[26] Perhaps most importantly of all, it can lead to a happier, more fulfilling life.

And that's not just of value to you personally; it's important for business as well. Businesses unable to generate big, disruptive, creative

23 Geoff Dyer, "Marathon Man," *The New York Times*, August 10, 2008, https://www.nytimes.com/2008/08/10/books/review/Dyer-t.html.

24 Mason Currey, "Tchaikovsky, Beethoven, Mahler: They All Loved Taking Long Daily Walks," *Slate*, April 25, 2013, https://slate.com/culture/2013/04/tchaikovsky-beethoven-mahler-they-all-loved-taking-long-daily-walks.html.

25 Sarah Moore, "What Is Neuronal Plasticity and Why Is It Important?" *News Medical*, December 12, 2019, https://www.news-medical.net/life-sciences/What-is-Neuronal-Plasticity-and-Why-Is-It-Important.aspx.

26 Nikki L. Hill et al., "Plasticity in Early Alzheimer's Disease: An Opportunity for Intervention," *Topics in Geriatric Rehabilitation* 27, no. 4 (2011): 257–67, https://doi.org/10.1097/tgr.0b013e31821e588e.

ideas eventually fail. It's in your company's interest, as much as yours, to find this time away.

All of which is to say, those Sundays you spend catching up on work or dashing around in a race to complete every chore for the entire week are doing real harm to your health, your career potential, and your enjoyment of your own life.

## Leave Room for More

I truly believe it's possible to reclaim our time for leisure. There are steps everyone can take, no matter their workload or position. I was once at a training for IBM executives in Somers, New York. I'd flown in from France, and other than the people I came with, I didn't really know anyone. Scanning the room, I wasn't sure how much I wanted to change that. The air was heavy with loud chatter and an undercurrent of intense competition. Everywhere around me, I saw high-octane type A personalities sizing up their competition, looking to devour one another.

Seeking refuge from the elite predators standing around the center of the room, I found a friendly looking, short old man sitting on his own. The main impression he made on me was that he seemed kind and welcoming. So, I sat down with him for a chat. Seeking a topic to get the conversation moving, I asked him about the hardest thing he'd dealt with in his career.

"Freeing up the time to think. I need two hours every day set aside for that. It took me a long while to secure that space for myself. My assistant used to pack my day with back-to-back meetings. That left no time to think. I had to really put my foot down on that. It became one of my nonnegotiables."

It was an interesting answer, but one that left me assuming he must be a lower-level executive of some sort in a creative department in the company. I couldn't imagine anyone who was actually important to operations could demand that kind of time in their schedule.

The sound of shuffling shoes and clinking plates set down in a hurry told us it was about time for the next presentation with the CEO to begin, so I excused myself. I found a seat in the front row and settled in. To my complete surprise, the elderly gentleman I'd just been talking to walked onto the stage. He introduced himself as Lou Gerstner, the CEO of IBM.

He began his speech with, "I was just talking to a member of our team from France, Shemin Nurmohamed, about how we can better use our time."

I learned two valuable lessons that day. First, don't assume you know what someone does based on a few details they drop about themselves. And second, if the CEO of IBM could carve out the time he needed to think and make unexpected connections, anyone could.

I've tried to live by both lessons. Despite now working at the higher end of the executive team at Pitney Bowes, I still make sure to leave most of my Sundays free of commitments. Even with the kids away at college, I get all my shopping and chores done on Friday and Saturday, so the day is free for a little rest and adventure.

This isn't as difficult as it might seem at first. To avoid a last-minute run to the grocery store, I keep a running shopping list of what I need as the week goes on and order everything in time to pick it up at my local Stop & Shop on Friday evening. If I go to a store on Sundays, it's for pleasure. I might go to Whole Foods for the ingredients for a meal I really want to cook, but I don't *have* to go.

Keeping lists and getting to chores early is a great start, but to really secure the time for leisure, you have to improve the structure around that time. Luckily, creating this space is easier than some of the recommendations in this book. For instance, getting more time for vacation can require switching jobs or making some uncomfortable demands from your employer. Freeing up time on the weekend and taking on new experiences is usually largely in your hands.

Make it known that you won't be available 24/7. Set boundaries around emails and texts on the weekend and after work hours. Even in my position, I'm able to set guidelines around communication on days off. I tell everyone on my team to choose their method of communication carefully. They can text me if it's urgent, and I'll respond. Everything else should be emailed, and that can wait until Monday. It means that if I do get a text, it had better be an emergency. This is, by the way, also a valuable boundary to set for your vacation time.

Also, you can find a partner to back you up during those days off. If work truly requires you to communicate over the weekend, take turns being the one responding for both of you. This is a win-win for you and your employer. It's better for business and better for you and your partner at work.

These boundaries and expectations can be shared straightforwardly. I have a one-page "how I work" document that allows everyone to understand my boundaries upfront—no risk of misunderstanding.

I don't just keep this rule for myself. I set that standard for everyone in the office. There are times when I might need to work on a Saturday, but that doesn't mean my team has to. If I send an email, I make it clear that I don't want my team to respond to me. Inevitably, someone new will try to respond once, perhaps assuming I don't mean what I say, but I don't respond back to them until Monday. Usually, they get the hint.

To avoid this, I often draft emails and schedule them to be sent on Monday morning. That way, there's no risk my team misinterprets my intentions.

As a leader, it's important to be mindful of the message you're sending through your own work habits. You may have times when you have to break your own boundaries and work beyond standard hours from time to time, but you can still protect the time of others. In our "work hard, play hard" American business environment, many assume that if the boss is working, they should be working too. But I have a lot more flexibility and ownership of my time during the week, and my kids are older. For those with younger families and more rigid weekly schedules, I am always mindful of their free time. I heard from senior executives at Warner Bros. Discovery that leadership often struggled to lead by example in this way. They have a "summer Fridays" program that allows workers to finish early on Fridays. After noon, there are supposed to be no calls and no meetings.

However, leaders at the company often used this quiet time to catch up on things such as emails, meaning all those people trying to leave early would end up staying late or even working weekends because they received communication from the top of the company.

This might have felt like light work for them, but it left others working harder during their time off. Eventually, the executives had to be told to stop emailing during this period so the policy could actually work as intended. According to a senior executive, this is now a great perk of working there.

This courtesy often pays dividends back when I am able to keep that Sunday free. My team knows I mean it when I tell them weekends are important, so they avoid bothering me as well.

Even on those weekends when I have to work, it's possible to engineer a little leisure and rest. I make sure to organize my time so that I can mostly focus on light work that I enjoy or that requires less mental strain. I'm fond of creative work such as marketing and product design. If we're under a tight deadline, I try to complete the stressful project work before Friday evening so I can enjoy the work I have left on Saturday.

As with everything, consistency wins in the end. Create a schedule, set boundaries, and determine accommodations that work for you, then stick to your plan. You may see some initial emails and requests come in those first few weekends, but with time, everyone will realize you're really taking that time for yourself. If it can work for Lou Gerstner, it can work for you.

Once you have that free time available, though, don't forget to use it to your advantage. The easiest thing in the world is to take that lazy Sunday and stay in, watching Netflix or scrolling social media. Instead, embrace the novel. Expand the smaller pieces of your pie. Take up chess; go for a long walk in the park. Have coffee with one friend in the morning and lunch with another in the afternoon.

These new adventures are available even if you don't have the Louvre nearby. Wherever you live, there are likely museums within a short distance of your home. Many of them have free days if you're on a budget. In fact, Bank of America has "free museum" weekends for its cardholders on the first weekend of every month. You can see some pretty impressive locations for free if you keep that weekend open. The Bruce Museum is next up on our list.

Your local public library is sure to be filled with events and clubs you could join. I'm a proud member of my library book club, for instance. My library also has movie nights and numerous hobbyist clubs that welcome newcomers. I'm sure yours does too.

When Fayyaz and I were younger, we were also fond of making an adventure out of the local bookstore. We'd choose a few potential purchases, investigate each for a bit, and then pick one book to take home with us.

No matter how small your town, there will be community events that you could join. Whether it's a weekend baseball league, a group of Sunday hikers, or a knitting class, there will be things you can try. All you have to do is sign up and show up.

And if you'd rather stay in, there is an unending number of books and YouTube videos that can teach you new skills. I've grown very fond of Jamie Oliver's fifteen-minute meals because I can try something new without a ton of prep or cooking time. You can go buy a Crock-Pot, look up some recipes, throw the ingredients in, and discover a new world of flavors.

No matter your interests or your schedule, the key to implementing these ideas really comes down to realizing how important a little changer d'air is and creating the space for it in your life.

## *La Vie Française in America*

Three ways to start living the French lifestyle today

1. The key to success in making the most of your time off is planning. Take an inventory of everything you do on the weekend. Be thorough. Categorize each activity and ask if there's a smarter way you could do it. Can you outsource some things (such as hiring a lawn care service) or do them more efficiently (such as shopping for groceries online)? For more on this, go to chapter 6.
2. Go to your local library or town hall, scan the list of activities in your area, and sign up for one that interests you. Even if it only meets once a month, start building a network of social connections around shared interests.
3. Look through the benefits offered by your work, credit cards, and community. See if any offer activities such as free museum visits, beach access, or park admittance. Choose one and go enjoy the experience with your family.

# CHAPTER 3

## Savor Every Meal

The lunch I detailed in the introduction was not actually my first experience with a French midday meal. Before I ever worked for IBM, I spent my first year in France as a chemistry teacher. As I prepared for the school year ahead, I remember marveling at how busy the cafés always were. All August, no matter the weather, every café was packed at lunchtime. Hungry customers would pool near the entrance, waiting for a table to free up. With the sound of English wafting up from many of the outdoor tables, I assumed the demand for a Parisian lunch was higher due to those last-minute travelers trying to taste the famous French cuisine before heading back to Britain or the States (and the fewer restaurants open).

As August lazily slid into September, I fully expected to see more empty tables and an overall quieter atmosphere—with the stillness of a college town once the students left for summer break. I was much surprised, then, when well into the autumn, I found every table just as occupied and reservations just as necessary.

I took particular notice of all this because I now had a stake in getting one of those tables. The school I worked at offered me and my fellow teachers an €8 lunch subsidy. This was essentially a coupon for lunch at the nearby café. This café, like most in Paris, had a prix fixe menu—a set-price meal with a limited number of options for each of your three courses. The total price for the meal was between €12 and €15. The subsidy allowed us to eat at half price—not a bad deal for a teacher eager to enjoy some of the famous French cuisine every afternoon.

For such a low price—no more than about $12 in America—you wouldn't believe how good the food was. French café fare is lighter and less plentiful than what we're used to on this side of the Atlantic. Appetizers were usually small and savory. One day, it might be a choice between six escargot or a small Caesar salad. The next day, it could be four shrimp with cocktail sauce, two mini kebabs, or a small quiche. For an entrée, you could often choose between two or three meat and fish options with a starch or vegetable on the side, such as braised lamb shank on a bed of wild rice, *poisson à la meunière* with mashed potatoes and capers, or *poulet confit* with a side of zucchini puree.

Dessert rounded out the lunch, my favorite part of the meal. The French are true lovers of pastries and all things sweet, and this is always on full display at a café. This particular café had seven types of chocolate cake, as well as coffee cake, *panna cotta*, and *café gourmand*: a dish that included three small desserts (such as a macaroon, a small piece of tiramisu, and a pistachio *financier*), served with coffee.

The meal would also include bread, already at the table when you arrived, and a glass of wine. The portions of all these delightful delicacies were small, many no larger than the top of a can of Coca-

Cola, and they were plated with the sort of artistic flourish we often associate with high-end restaurants in the States.

Despite the beautiful, delicious food on display, the cuisine was not the biggest difference I noticed from my lunch experiences in America and Canada; it was how the French ate lunch. In France, lunch was an event, a nearly two-hour enterprise. It took ten minutes to walk from the school to the café. Ten minutes to wait for our table. Ten minutes to get the attention of the *serveur* and order. And after lunch was complete, it took ten minutes to walk back. In between, we spent about an hour on lunch itself.

That hour was spent in joyful conversation with colleagues or sometimes quiet relaxation. I've always appreciated that the French are equally comfortable eating in large groups or alone. At one table, you might find a lively conversation about French politics and at the next, a woman reading a book quietly on her own.

That's what made these meals so special. It was an opportunity to slow down and really savor the moment as much as the food. Instead of rushing to the next bite as soon as they're done swallowing the last one, French people put their utensils down, chew fully, and use their free hands to gesticulate while they talk. The entire meal is an experience, one that no one is eager to rush.

## A Healthier Déjeuner

This leisurely approach to lunch stands in stark contrast to how we treat our midday meals across the Atlantic. In North America, we optimize lunch. The general attitude here is that lunch is a time we should aim to shrink down until it barely exists. In one 2015 study, fewer than 20 percent of American workers left their place of employment for lunch. That same study found that 39 percent just ate at their desks.[27] And this was before Uber Eats launched across the country. An incredible 48 percent of workers say they skip at least one lunch a week outright.[28]

For many, lunch is not seen as an opportunity to recharge or enjoy a meal; it's framed in terms of lost productivity. The sooner it's over, the better. And that leads to many negative consequences. We've already seen in the last chapter the importance of stepping away and engaging in leisure activities for creativity and clear thinking. The same is true on the scale of lunch and a single workday. Sitting in the same place without a break doesn't make us more productive; it makes us less so.[29] You don't need a study to prove this, though. Just look at your Fitbit or Oura Ring, which prompts you to get up every hour—including the lunch hour. This is because it's just healthier to move around for a bit, and going to lunch outside the office accomplishes this.

Moving around aside, staying at our desks also encourages us to eat less healthily. The vast majority of us tend to gravitate toward highly processed foods we can heat up in a minute in a microwave over better options that might take more time.[30]

---

27 Ellie Krieger, "You May Look More Productive Skipping Lunch, or Eating at Your Desk. But You Aren't," *The Washington Post*, November 10, 2015, https://www.washingtonpost.com/lifestyle/wellness/take-a-lunch-break-to-do-better-work/2015/11/05/0a33869e-8275-11e5-a7ca-6ab6ec20f839_story.html.

28 Jess Cording, "New Survey Shows Many Workers Aren't Taking a Lunch Break," *Forbes*, December 12, 2023, https://www.forbes.com/sites/jesscording/2023/12/12/new-survey-shows-many-workers-arent-taking-a-lunch-break/.

29 Christine Bosch et al., "What Makes for a Good Break? A Diary Study on Recovery Experiences During Lunch Break," *Journal of Occupational and Organizational Psychology* 91, no. 1 (2017): 134–157, https://doi.org/10.1111/joop.12195.

30 Courtney Rehfeldt, "American Workers May Be Eating Their Way to Poor Productivity," *Athletech News*, May 20, 2024, https://athletechnews.com/americans-workplace-eating-habits-ultra-processed-foods-lifesum/.

In contrast, the French approach to *le déjeuner* has enormous benefits to your individual health and personal life. The French focus on savoring healthy, unprocessed food, fostering social connections, and taking a break from work all offer clear positives for a healthier, happier life. For instance, because they savor every bite, the French eat their smaller, heartier portions more slowly. Slowing down over a meal reduces how much you need to eat to feel full.[31] And you stay full longer. I hardly ever saw a French person snack the entire time I was in the country—apart from the obligatory goûter (snack) for school kids around three in the afternoon.

These dietary changes can have serious effects on our mental and physical health. We live in a country that struggles with obesity, and France offers at least part of the solution. Even as its own obesity rates have risen in recent years, France still has a rate less than half that of America and significantly lower than that of its neighbor, Britain.[32] Diet plays a huge part in this. In the introduction, I mentioned my friend Laura Miragoli, who could easily have been a supermodel. I always marveled at how slender and healthy she looked. But when I asked about her workout routine one day, she simply laughed. She didn't have one; she just ate well.

This same pattern maps onto long-term health concerns. I think it's no coincidence that France has half as many cases of diabetes per capita as America.[33]

---

31 Franziska Spritzler, "Does Eating Slowly Help You Lose Weight?" *Healthline*, June 18, 2019, https://www.healthline.com/nutrition/eating-slowly-and-weight-loss#eating-slowly.

32 "France Sees a Surprising Surge in Obesity," *The Economist*, January 26, 2023, https://www.economist.com/europe/2023/01/26/france-sees-a-surprising-surge-in-obesity.

33 Alberto Rojo Moro, "Mapped: Diabetes Rates by Country in 2021," *Visual Capitalist*, May 27, 2023, https://www.visualcapitalist.com/cp/diabetes-rates-by-country/.

Our eating habits don't just affect our physical health; they also play a role in our general emotional state. Americans tend to eat bad food quickly, which leads to a short-term glucose spike. Once the spike recedes, we feel hungry again. That's when we reach for a snack. If we can't get to one in time, we all know what happens next: We get "hangry." We're annoyed by everything because our glucose levels are too low. We end up snapping at a team member, or arguing with our spouse when we get home, precisely because we rushed through a hamburger at our desk. In one study, married couples were given pins and voodoo dolls to test their emotional tolerance for one another. Each pin represented an aggressive impulse toward their partner. Those whose glucose levels spiked and then dipped dramatically stuck in far more pins than the others.[34]

Eating whole foods, eating more vegetables, and eating everything more slowly allows the glucose levels to remain steady, providing constant energy for longer. We don't end up hangry, because our bodies are nourished.

As we can see, then, body and mind are better cared for with a better lunch—and so is the soul. Taking the time to sit down to a midday meal with colleagues can create real, lasting relationships. Many of my closest friendships have begun in work canteens. Most of these were built over several years of regular lunch encounters. The French are friendly and polite, but friendships aren't made instantly in the way that they are in North America (where they also tend to be more fleeting—no coincidence). Instead, they take their time opening up over the course of many interactions and shared experiences.

---

34 Yogi Patel, "Voodoo Dolls Show How Hunger and Lack of Self-Control Go Hand in Hand," *Ars Technica*, April 18, 2014, https://arstechnica.com/science/2014/04/voodoo-dolls-show-how-hunger-and-lack-of-self-control-go-hand-in-hand/.

Sharing a meal together doesn't guarantee friendship, but it makes it more possible. And in this era of loneliness, that benefit shouldn't be ignored.

## The Value of a Good Business Lunch

Considering all these benefits, it's no wonder the French feel le déjeuner is almost as sacred as taking Sunday off. It's a big, important meal—one that deserves time and respect. It's so respected, in fact, that many French businesses used to close at lunchtime so the employees could either have a sit-down meal together or go home to eat with their families (the busy, modern world has sadly mostly erased this tradition at this point). But that doesn't mean there are no business benefits to this policy. In reality, a French lunch is also a valuable tool for achieving business aims.

Throughout my time at IBM, across several different roles, I noticed that many of the best salespeople opted to do their business over lunch instead of in the office or over dinner. A lot of things don't get said in the boardroom. Whether it's an issue with company politics or a general feeling that sharing certain information might be considered disloyal to their company, many potential clients keep the conversation too formal to actually close a sale. These same potential clients, though, can become far more open over lunch, particularly if a salesperson takes time to build a relationship over those meals.

I've experienced this myself. I was at one of my favorite places, *Le Relais de Venise*, the original entrecôte restaurant, with steaks so good, it always had a long queue of hopeful diners snaking around the corner of the street, rain or shine. Inside, the tables were bunched so closely together that your arm might accidentally touch your neighbor's as you cut into that perfect piece of beef. The close quarters meant you'd inevitably overhear conversations at nearby tables, and it was perfectly normal to start a companionable chat with someone a few feet to your left or right. It was there that I once wound up sitting next to the CTO of a company we had been trying to create a partnership with. Our discussions had hit a snag, and the whole deal was stalled. But that changed over lunch. I recognized the CTO's face and reintroduced myself. After accidentally spilling water on him like a complete klutz (or perhaps an unintentionally brilliant salesperson), I also managed an introduction with his CEO. The three of us started talking, and we wound up arranging a meeting. The relationship led to one of my department's bigger deals that year, which got quoted in the earnings release.

These lunches create wonderful networking opportunities, and that isn't just true when dining at elite French restaurants. The French corporate canteen is also full of opportunities to meet colleagues and forge new connections. The canteen is a very democratic place. Unlike a school cafeteria, it isn't cliquey. Most people go to lunch alone and simply find a spot at one of the large, long tables where all are welcome, regardless of position or department. The presiding atmosphere is friendly and inviting. Lunch is an opportunity to talk to staff from other parts of the business, sparking conversations that wouldn't happen elsewhere, without the pressure of performing that is present in the office. This is how informal networks form, and it's the place where a chance introduction or a scrap of shared information might just make the difference in a key decision.

These richer social networks at work foster a more positive work environment, improve employee morale, and enhance social connections among colleagues. This can lead to better collaboration, teamwork, and overall job satisfaction.[35] I've long suspected that the main reason Americans skip lunch is not actually about their ambitions to be more productive; it's about their desire to get away from work as soon as possible. Their workplace makes them unhappy, so they'd rather suffer through a missed meal than stay a minute later at the office. According to this way of thinking, a little starvation is a small price to pay for ducking out twenty minutes early. With longer, more social, healthier lunches, though, work becomes more bearable, even enjoyable. With a real break in the day, more people will take the time to enjoy that opportunity instead of focusing on the break that comes at the end of their shift.

Whether it's closing a deal, building a new connection, or strengthening relationships on the team, lunch can be good business when it's run the French way.

## Scheduling Shared Meals

Even if you aren't looking to make a sale or talk over a major project, sharing time together over a meal is a great way to build stronger relationships. That's not to say there's anything wrong with eating lunch alone. That's a common, and often positive, way to recharge. But on occasion, it's worthwhile to take that time and share a meal with others at work. And you don't need a French cafeteria to create space for these interactions. If you're in the position to arrange schedules, you can set times, locations, and expectations for shared meals with those on your team.

---

35 Casey Conway, "Lunch Is Served! Workplace Meals Improve Productivity," *Business News Daily*, October 24, 2023, https://www.businessnewsdaily.com/8638-employees-eat-together.html.

I make a point of having lunch with every new person who joins my department. It's a chance to get to know one another. I also have regular checkup lunches to see how each member of the team is doing—particularly those I haven't seen face-to-face in a few weeks. While work is necessarily part of the conversation, we spend a lot of our time on more informal, personal topics. We talk about family and shared interests. Do they have a dog? How old are their kids? Where did they go on their last vacation? What sport do they follow? What team do they support?

This is the stuff that really matters to people, and when you create space to talk about it over a meal, you let them know that in that context, you're meeting as equals. You can create a space for informality, a place where you're all just people curious about one another. These moments of genuine connection pave the way for deeper, stronger relationships over time, reinforced by those points of common interest.

To create that openness, I schedule these lunches for an hour to ninety minutes, depending on schedules and deadlines. That way, no one is in a rush. We can take our time and find our way to connection. This pays dividends in lower attrition, as the team knows that their manager sees them. It also improves alignment because we spend much of the time digging into why we're pursuing a particular strategy. And it lowers the number of sick days because I'm able to keep track of the workload and bandwidth for the people on my team.

Perhaps the most valuable benefit of these informal lunches emerges in how they transform workplace communication. As I'll cover in more detail in chapter 8, the informality and trust built by these shared meals allow for another important component of communication that's often missing in the US business context: contradiction. The French love a debate. They relish challenging conversations. Contradicting a colleague isn't automatically perceived as threatening or undermining in the way it would likely be in the US or Canada. This makes for a refreshing work culture and a lot of interesting and stimulating lunchtime discussions. When contradiction loses its sting—when it stops seeming like insubordination or conflict—better ideas get expressed, and points of disagreement get aired instead of buried.

These points of disagreement might be anything from music to a work project the team is trying to get off the ground. Once everyone is comfortable sharing their opinions, you can leverage that openness to improve your own work. I often use my colleagues' reactions as a barometer when I'm trying to gauge whether a new approach is worth pursuing. I can honestly say I've received some of my best work advice over lunch, gaining fresh perspective from the most unexpected quarters.

Good food, good people, and good advice all in one. What could be better?

## Eating Better in the Fast-Food Capital of the World

With so many business benefits, you'd think America would already be on board with the French preference for longer, healthier lunches. Yet despite these clear advantages, our workplace culture continues to push in the opposite direction, creating both personal and social pressure to eat faster and cheaper each day. So, how do we create the space for a better lunch in the mad rush of North American business culture?

The answer comes in two parts: how we eat and what we do with our time.

Eating better starts with reframing how we think about food. To maximize the benefits we receive from our lunch, we can reframe the meal into an exercise in mindfulness. No matter how much time you have to eat, you can focus on slowing down and savoring each bite. Instead of downing an entire chocolate bar, concentrate on an individual piece; let it melt in your mouth.

As you enjoy each bite, increase that mindfulness by creating the conditions for focus. Don't multitask. Staring at a screen while you eat leads to shoveling food in automatically. It can also raise your stress levels. If you're working through lunch, you aren't getting any of the benefits that come from stepping away and recharging. Instead, close the laptop, put the phone away, and just sit and enjoy your food.

Ultimately, lunch should be an event in your day, and you are entirely in charge of whether you see it that way or not. Even when I'm eating alone, I leave my desk and go to the conference table. I put away all my technology, and I use a knife and fork. I make it matter, a point of departure from the rest of the day. I also like to keep a notepad and a pen nearby in case I have a good idea. Instead of a moment to catch up on more work, it can be a chance to open myself up to those creative forces that increase when we step away from work tasks.

You are also likely in charge of what you eat. The default options may be unhealthy, but you can change the default. Your gut has a greater impact on your quality of life than you may realize, so treat it better. Change up your meals to be more nutritionally rich and varied. Eating the same boring sandwich every day, stuffed with nutritionally poor contents, is bad news for your gut. People who eat the most varied diets have a more diverse and healthy gut flora. This is an important measure of health, as a lack of good bacteria has been linked with everything from depression to weight gain.

This doesn't mean you have to become a great chef. You can look out for healthier places to eat that offer better options. You might be surprised how many restaurants have menus that provide better lunch options. In my little, relatively small town, we have a restaurant that has a prix fixe menu. The portions are much larger than what you'd encounter in France—they're two meals in one for me—but at $27 for two meals, it's not a bad price for good food.

There are also many services these days that will ship you healthy food you can make for lunch. They often require nothing more than the same microwave you were already using to heat up those highly processed meals you've been eating for years.

One final way you can reframe your thinking around what you're eating is education. In particular, I recommend *The Glucose Revolution* by Jessie Inchauspé. In the third part of that book, Inchauspé includes ten "hacks" to reduce those harmful glucose spikes. They include easy adjustments to your diet, such as eating your vegetables first and walking for five minutes after you eat. Even a few small changes can make an impact. It's a great start toward a better way of eating.

With a few modest adjustments, you might be surprised how quickly you start eating better—and feeling better. And that can help in your career and your personal life. When you have more energy and focus—when you're able to slow down and enjoy a meal—that's when you can really begin to savor and take full advantage of each moment.

## *La Vie Française in America*

Three ways to start living the French lifestyle today

1. Schedule time in your calendar for lunch. This could start with as little as fifteen minutes that you slowly increase to thirty over a few weeks or months, but that time should be set aside. During this time, change your location—whether you go out to eat or just go to a different room. If you can't change your location, at least turn off the computer and put your phone somewhere you can't reach for it.
2. Make a point of getting to know one person over lunch. This could be someone in your department or on your floor. Walk to lunch together and eat together. If you brought your lunch, find someone who did the same. You can expand from there. When I did this, I ended up creating networks for people who had been working a few doors down from one another for years without much contact.
3. Apply at least four of the ten *The Glucose Revolution* tips for each meal.

# CHAPTER 4

## C'est la Vie

In 2012, I stepped into a completely new world in my career. I took over as the leader of IBM's sales team responsible for hardware sales to a European Other Equipment Manufacturer.[36] I'd never worked a day in sales in my life. Actually, that's not true. I had, in fact, one single day of sales experience. To make this new role all the more intimidating, I was taking over a mature, very effective team that was already doing well; they just weren't hitting their aggressive targets. They already had the right relationships, and they already had the right skills. For some reason, my American bosses thought I'd be able to push them that little bit further to hit their numbers. But with a limited knowledge of sales, what exactly was I supposed to offer?

It would have been easy for my new team to dismiss me. Perhaps they had all already enjoyed rolling their eyes when they heard about

36 An Other Equipment Manufacturer is a company that produces parts and equipment that are then incorporated into the products of other companies.

my appointment. Instead of avoiding that topic, though, I decided to steer my opening remarks right into it.

"You probably think this is some kind of joke," I told them. "Some experiment to see if a random executive will sink or swim when they completely change roles. But while we all see how this plays out, I have a proposition for you. I want to make your lives easier. So, if you show me how you do your calls and take me when you go meet clients, I'll do the pricing of your deal for you and get it approved by accounting."

This proposal allowed me to leverage one of the few things I knew about sales: Salespeople hate the financial side of their work. Pricing often comes down to how you word things. Get the wording wrong, and a part of a sale might not count as revenue—and that's a problem for a salesperson who is compensated based on the revenue they generate. Since I'd come from finance, I knew all the secrets in this area. It was a natural alliance, one that could get me up to speed while helping remove the biggest burden from the entire team.

The first person who volunteered for this partnership was Remi Morillon. With close-cut gray hair and intelligent brown eyes, Remi was the department's highflier. He was a master of his craft and watching him work with a client was a true pleasure—like watching Rodin shaping marble with his deft chisel. The most interesting thing I learned from Remi, though, wasn't his technique in front of the client; it was his view on life. Every time he took me to a client, he would tell me their story. He understood clients in terms of their lives and the interests and preferences they'd shared about themselves. The stories of these interests had nothing to do with IBM hardware or the demands of the client's industry—they were about their lives beyond the office.

Remi had realized long ago that he and a client could always find a joint passion for something outside of work. That was because

Remi had more interests than you could imagine. Whether it was wine tasting, golfing, or hiking, there was something important in the client's life, a place with far more passion than their position at work, and Remi probably shared it.

Sometime later, when I was well established in my role and comfortable with the world of sales, I spoke to Remi about his upcoming retirement. I was used to the American experience of senior people in every organization clinging on to their positions as long as possible. Remi, though, wasn't depressed or desperate to stay. Far from fearing retirement or worrying about all the free time he'd have, he embraced the change. I found it fascinating, so I asked him about it. Why was he so excited to stop working?

With a gentle shrug, he told me, "I have all these other pieces of my life that I've seeded and nurtured over the course of my life. Now, I'll get to spend more time on those pieces. Maybe I'll even add another thing or two."

Retirement didn't mean he was losing a step. It was just leaving behind one part of his life to focus on all the others. In particular, he had a nonprofit for refugees that he ran. Retirement wasn't the end of his work; it was a shift to a different kind of work. And he would have plenty to keep him busy.

## What Is Work?

Remi's approach to life and work reflected a distinctly French perspective that stands in sharp contrast to how we view these relationships in America. In America, work is everything. The only thing that counts as work—as deserving that concept—is the job you hold. In other words, there's "work," and there's "personal," and work often gets the lion's share of the time and attention. If you're lucky enough to work in an area that you're passionate about, this can be an overall pleasant arrangement. You can define yourself by that work and feel good about yourself. Maybe you always wanted to be a doctor. Once you're an MD, working those long hours is mostly satisfying and reaffirming. Writers, musicians, artists, and entrepreneurs are often fueled by the passion they feel for their careers. Many would continue to do their work even if they didn't need the money.

That's wonderful, but the majority of people work because they have to. For them, that singular focus is a clear drag on their quality of life. With little joy in the work and little time for anything else, life can begin to feel empty quickly. Even for those who love their job, there's a real weakness in relying upon work for most of your meaning in life. When work is everything, you become dependent on it. Losing a job becomes more than a financial strain; it's a loss of identity. It becomes difficult to ever walk away—whether for a weekend or for the rest of your life.

The truth is we do have two sides to life, but it's not work and personal. According to a popular saying, "We have two lives; the second begins when we realize we only have one." In other words, real life begins when you truly understand you only have so much time. Your life includes work, but it shouldn't be limited to it. And limiting your own perspective that way can only do harm.

This is why the French work fewer hours—usually around thirty-five a week for labor and a little over forty hours for management and other white-collar work.[37] They take this extra time and invest it in the rest of their lives. While they are just as productive in their work, they make a point of spending time away from the office on the things they

37 Peter Weber, "France Aspires to Work by Working Less. Is It Working?" *The Week*, March 29, 2023, https://theweek.com/in-depth/1022073/france-aspires-to-work-by-working-less-is-it-working.

care most about—the stuff they feel really matters. They get season tickets to the opera. They work out. They go to their kid's football games.[38] Even vacation becomes more than just time away from work. It transforms into a year-round source of joy as people spend months anticipating and planning their trips, savoring the experience long before they ever leave home. They spend months reading about and planning a trip. The trip becomes a whole source of pleasure and excitement well before they can take the time off. All of this makes life richer, more interesting, and more fulfilling.

In essence, the French long ago realized that life isn't about work–life balance; it's about life–work balance. Instead of feeling that work always has to come first, they give life more of a priority. There's no reason to feel guilty at home, away from work. And once you give more of your attention to life—once you increase the size of those pieces of your pie—you may find you don't feel guilty at work for being away from home either. If you do this right, work remains important; it's just not overwhelming the whole pie. I had neighbors in France whom I became friends with, and I didn't know what they did for work. The topic never came up because we had so many other things to talk about.

Getting this balance right every day is impossible. There will be moments with a lot of freedom to invest in life and moments that demand a lot of work. But if you keep that new order of priority in mind, over time, you'll find a better balance, which can only be good for your life and your work.

## Increasing Resilience

One of the reasons American workers tend to fear retirement so much is that they have little beyond work in their lives. Many spend the

38 That's soccer over here in North America.

entire length of their careers living the vast majority of their waking hours at work. What time is left goes to family—with perhaps a few hours left for friends and other activities. By the time most people retire, their kids are grown and living their own lives. Friends have come and gone. Working long hours without investing in other interests leaves these future retirees feeling their entire identity is constructed around their job—and losing that is terrifying. This singular focus on work leaves us unprepared for the natural shifts in life and the inevitable setbacks we will face. We lose all resilience because there's nothing else in our lives to draw energy and validation from. If we aren't working, what are we?

To increase our level of resilience, we have to invest in those areas of interest and validation that come from beyond our job title. There are so many sources of validation available in life: family, friendships, and hobbies, to name just a few. You can focus more time on travel or do as Remi did and put your efforts into volunteering. It isn't important *what* you do; it's that you increase the balance between your priorities.

With more balance in how we validate ourselves, we naturally grow more resilient. When things go wrong, it doesn't mean everything has to go wrong. If you have ten priorities in your life, when two go wrong, you still have eight you can rely on. If you miss out on a promotion, you can still have your daughter's choir concert to look forward to, as well as the mountain biking trip you've planned with a couple of old friends and the charity event you're attending over the weekend. This robustness in life can allow you to weather the tough moments until you can see the opportunity at the end of the storm.

And that opportunity will come. This philosophy of building a life beyond your primary career was beautifully articulated by Roger

Federer in his graduation speech at Dartmouth in 2024.[39] Early in the speech, he spoke about how he rejected the word *retired*, instead seeing the end of his tennis career as a graduation, having "finished one big thing" and "moving on to the next." Even as he admitted that he didn't know what his next step was, he spoke of all the things that still filled his life. He took care of his kids. He played chess online. He cleaned the house.

He attributed much of his success to those parts of his life that hardly touched on tennis. As he put it, "I knew that tennis could show me the world … but tennis could never be the world." Even when he was at the top, he prioritized having a "rewarding life, full of travel, culture, friendships, and especially family." He also focused on giving back by starting a foundation to empower children through education.

His life, in other words, helped him reach the top, and it made him resilient when he faced adversity. In that same speech, he spoke about struggles early in his career to remain focused and reach his full potential. Part of what allowed him to move beyond those early setbacks was the people in his life. He was able to do all that he did partly because of the lesson he closed his speech with: "Life is bigger than the court."

## A Different Kind of Focus

Across his entire career, Federer won about 80 percent of his matches, but he only won 54 percent of the points. What separated him from other players—beyond his obvious talent—was his ability to focus on the next point. He could put the past behind him, refuse

---

39 Roger Federer, "2024 Commencement Address by Roger Federer at Dartmouth," posted June 9, 2024, by Dartmouth, YouTube, 14 min., 31 sec., https://www.youtube.com/watch?v=pqWUuYTcG-o.

to dwell on the lost point, and focus on the next one. Each point, at the moment it's being played, is the most important one. When it's past, it's better forgotten.

It takes incredible mental resilience to make those margins work for you. Forty-six percent of the time, Federer did everything he could, and he still lost the point. What made him great—and allowed him to have one of the greatest careers in tennis history—was his ability to move beyond the difficult moments and see the new opportunity in front of him.

And while he didn't tie this directly to the depth of support he had from the rest of his life, I think it's hard to see the two as disconnected.

Perhaps counterintuitively, investing in life often bears fruit in work like this. Consider two salespeople. One is like Remi, a master salesperson with a rich life beyond his work. The other is your traditional, competitive seller with a singular focus on getting the win. A salesperson like Remi goes into a client meeting as prepared for a sale as the other salesperson—but their motivation isn't solely on that sale. They see themselves as experts, ready to assist and eager for a good conversation. It's a consultative approach, one in which they are happy to offer several options because they're confident they have the best one in hand. A missed sale is a disappointment, but it isn't crushing.

The other salesperson, though, is driven solely by the need for validation in their work. They don't take no for an answer because their ego can't afford to. They may start their pitch the same way as Remi, but as soon as it looks like they're losing the client, they turn aggressive, drop the niceties, and launch into the hard sale.

I think we all know intuitively which salesperson will ultimately be more successful. I think we all know who ends up being happier as well.

I've experienced this in my own career. I didn't just have to find resilience when moving into sales without any experience. When I first came to work at Pitney Bowes, I joined with an eye on the executive vice president of International Sales role. Soon after settling in, though, I discovered that the person currently in that position had no intention of leaving. Making matters even more difficult, many others in the organization had their eye on the same role. If I invested everything into getting that position, I would have been locked in a frustrating struggle that benefited no one. Instead, I focused on the work at hand and the other interests in my life, and I left myself open to other possibilities.

In the end, through a series of fortunate events, I never got the executive vice president of International Sales role. I became the president of Global Business instead. The other role was dissolved in the new organization.

## The Power of Gratitude

One unspoken value in Federer's speech was the importance of gratitude. He was grateful for his career. Grateful for his success. Grateful for family, friends, and incredible experiences. He was clearly grateful to be at Dartmouth that day, despite the rain. His gratitude extended to every aspect of life, including that very moment at Dartmouth. Despite his extraordinary success, he remained genuinely thankful for the honorary doctorate he was receiving—a particularly meaningful recognition for someone who had never attended college himself.

Gratitude can sound like a throwaway concept in our hard-nosed business world. Focusing on it can almost feel like empty new age nonsense. But one of the best ways to increase resilience is to recognize all the good things we already have in life. You may not have all the hobbies you would like. You may not have enough time to train for a marathon like you've always wanted. But you may have a good group of friends or a great trip planned for next summer. You may have kids, a spouse, or a couple of dogs. All that gratitude is, at its root, is simply recognizing how good it is to have those things in your life. And by focusing attention on that, we can become happier, healthier, and more resilient. That's no exaggeration; studies have found that gratitude can improve our immune system, calm our nervous system, and boost our circulatory system.[40]

It also makes it easier for us to focus on living in whatever moment we're in. We can be grateful for our work and motivated to do well in our job, and we can be grateful for our lazy Sunday with family, the extended lunch with friends, or the wonderful vacation we're taking to some faraway place.

Life is so much more pleasant when we focus on what is wonderful in the here and now. There is an apocryphal—but still accurate—quote, "If you are depressed you are living in the past. If you are anxious you are living in the future. If you are at peace you are living in the present."

When we are grateful for our present, we can thrive in that present and build upon that present. We can seek out more of what makes that present worth living in across every aspect of our lives.

## Pause and Reflect

My daughter recently shared a fact about graduate students with me. Around 90 percent of those who took a gap year—a year away from academic work—before applying for their PhD never returned to

---

40 Misty Pratt, "The Science of Gratitude," *Mindful*, February 17, 2022, https://www.mindful.org/the-science-of-gratitude/.

academia.[41] It's a shockingly high number, but I don't think it's that surprising. So often, we don't know what we want until we've had a little time to have some new experiences and then a little more time to slow down and figure things out.

I had enrolled in university assuming I'd become a doctor. Growing up, my family suggested there were only two paths to success: I could be a lawyer or a doctor. Law didn't interest me at all, so I figured I'd have to go into medicine. As a premed, I studied chemistry. I took all the exams. I was just blindly following that path, until one day, in the midst of a clearly unenthusiastic conversation about my future career, a friend of mine pulled me up short.

"Wait a minute," she said. "Do you even want to be a doctor?"

The answer must have been written across my face.

This is one of the reasons I prefer the American education system to the French one. In France, young people are pushed into a narrow set of choices for their careers from very early in life. It becomes incredibly difficult to redefine yourself. This is why I had such a hard time working in finance in France at first. Every French company saw that I had a chemistry degree and refused to give me a chance. It took IBM, an American company, to offer me an opportunity.

In our moments of unhappiness, when we lack the robustness of life I've described in this chapter, the best thing we can do is pause, examine ourselves, and figure out what we're missing. Whenever an employee comes to me asking for more money, I always slow the conversation down. I take a step back and look at the root cause of this request. Almost always, the employee's motivation comes from one of three sources. In the first place, they might be trying to climb too quickly. They're career obsessed and want to reach the top faster

---

41 "What Gap Year Statistics Tell Us About the Impact of Gap Year Programs on College Success," *NOLS*, May 15, 2023, https://blog.nols.edu/what-gap-year-statistics-tell-us.

than anyone else. If they're paid well for the work they're producing for the company, I tell them to go ahead and look around for a better role. When they struggle to find something better, they often reset, realizing there's more to do before they can rise higher.

The second reason someone asks for more money is that they lack an interest in their work. They're doing well, but they need help finding purpose in what they do. Essentially, they're bored and unmotivated. This might be because they need help finding inspiration in their role or it might be a need for more interests in the rest of their life. I try to help them with the former and encourage them to seek the latter themselves.

Finally, employees come to me about their paychecks because they're worried about their future. They're critical to the company, but they just haven't bought into the company's vision yet. They don't see how they can grow with the company. With a little reassurance about what their future might look like and more focus on the present, we can usually find a resolution.

In each of these situations, the only way to reach a solution is through pausing and considering the reality of the person sitting across from me. And that's the case no matter how you feel about your life–work balance right now. However full or busy your life feels at the moment, there's always value in slowing down for a bit and engaging in some self-reflection.

You don't have to wait for an important birthday to review the course of your life. I schedule a reflection period at the end of every December, just as we're heading into the holidays. Can I live with the regrets of the choices I've taken this past year, as well as the regrets of the choices I've not taken? Am I getting value out of the life I'm living? This is a chance to disengage the autopilot and ask myself some tough questions.

The French often make this a social act. They'll ask these questions of their social circle. When they go out to dinner, they skip the pleasantries and focus on more philosophical conversation, seeking deeper answers about life. The aim is to avoid coasting, making sure their current path is the right one for them.

Whether done alone or with friends, the exercise has value. We'd all like to end up like Remi, happy regardless of whether we're going to keep working or retire—because life is full either way.

---

## *La Vie Française in America*

Three ways to start living the French lifestyle today

1. Do a reality check of your life priorities. Draw a pie with four to eight slices. Give each slice a name for an important area of your life: work, family, spirituality, health, hobbies, etc. Look at the last three months of your calendar. Assess the volume of time spent on each. Now redraw the pie to accurately reflect how you spend your time. Is this pie reflective of how you want to spend your time? If so, great. Redraw the pie every six months to double-check that you're still on track. If not, pick one piece of pie you want to improve upon and make time for it in your calendar.
2. Pick a week when you'll be meeting a lot of new people. Try to have a conversation without bringing up work.
3. Pick one area of interest and invest more time exploring it. Find a series of books on the topic or a podcast you can listen to.

---

# CHAPTER 5

## Cultivating Expertise

I took my time getting to the top of my profession, but in France, that slow, winding career path wasn't an anomaly. I was surrounded by leaders who had chosen to move laterally across disciplines related to their expertise, building knowledge before moving vertically.

That was certainly the way I'd describe the career of my friend Xavier Vasques. Elegantly dressed, with glasses and an easy smile (a rare quality in a French person), Xavier started with IBM as a deep computing specialist, but he got his start at AXA, an insurance company, where he worked as a mathematician. In America, he probably would have sought a higher-paying position in mathematics at another insurance company. Instead, he left AXA to study for his PhD at the prestigious Centre national de la recherche scientifique, where he used his mathematical models in functional genomics.

You might assume that his next move would be into professorship or perhaps back to insurance, where he could move swiftly into leadership. Instead, that's when he decided to go to IBM, where, over the next few years, he moved between several roles. Over five years, he went from deep computing specialist to data analytics and finally manager of the innovation lab. Instead of continuing up, though, he left IBM for the École Polytechnique Fédérale de Lausanne in Switzerland and worked as a researcher and manager there.

In total, it was about a decade before he really started taking a more direct vertical path up the ladder. For many on this side of the Atlantic, such a slow process would seem a waste of time. But Xavier had used that winding path to his advantage. Over all those years, he'd become a masterful communicator. With all his research across so many positions, he'd become adept at absorbing complex ideas and simplifying and explaining them to the layperson.

Xavier was always more interested and curious in the person he was speaking to than proving he was the smartest person in the room—and that brought a lot of advantages to his communication. That easy smile came with the skill to make the complicated seem easy and approachable. Across his many positions, he'd gone to countless conferences and come back to summarize what he'd learned. Doing that so many times, practicing that skill with so many different people, he'd learned to grade his speech based on his audience. And that gave him a skill that sent him straight to the top. By the time I left the company, he had gone gray at the temples, but he'd also risen to CTO for IBM France.

## Straight Up Isn't Always Best

Xavier's meandering yet purposeful career path exemplifies a fundamentally different approach to professional growth than what we typically see in American business culture. The American approach to career advancement is all about speed. It's a race to the top of the ladder, climbing each rung any way possible, so long as you get there before everyone else. This obsession with speed at all costs necessarily precludes any focus on qualification, experience, study, or preparation. There's no room to build a sturdy foundation; that just slows you down. It's all about aiming for the stars and getting there quickly.

This philosophy has its obvious benefits. You get to the top of your profession without having to wait so long. That earns you the prestige of the top title and the pay grade to back it up. More money, more power, more importance, all at the earliest possible age—what's not to like?

When you step back from your ambitions a bit, though, this worldview brings with it a lot of problems. In particular, it leads to stress, strain on the rest of your life, and significant risk to your overall career path.

There's a reason Americans struggle so much with imposter syndrome: They've often advanced faster than their experience and the depth of their understanding. Instead of slowing down and developing the knowledge necessary for a higher position, they grasp at every promotion on offer. This often means they jump from company to company, losing the support and guidance of colleagues as they go, all to get that next title and the next bump in pay.

But rising so quickly makes it harder to hold on to those gains. Moving up to a position you aren't prepared for without allies to support you leaves you exposed as the top candidate for replacement when it's time to shake things up. You stick out as the highest-paid and least effective worker in your area.

I speak from experience. I have been involved in over seven major restructurings during my time at IBM and Pitney Bowes. The first place we always look when considering who to let go is senior leadership. These are the most expensive positions, and often, a subordinate one position below actually knows more than the person holding the job. In other words, if the person in the top job rose too quickly and lacks the depth of experience and knowledge to make them irreplaceable, when you have to cut payroll costs, letting them go is the easiest, most obvious choice.

There's also a more personal risk attached to getting promoted too soon. Changing out houses and cars every couple of years in an effort to keep up with your new income is not just wasteful—it's risky. Instead of saving and carefully considering where you want to live and what you want to drive, you can end up throwing money around just because you have it. But that behavior leads to significant debts, which in turn require you to keep moving up to pay them off.

In France, workers usually take the opposite perspective. They value building a foundation of knowledge. They progress more slowly, but that also means they don't overshoot their current abilities by rising above their knowledge level. It's rare for French people to leave companies. Like Xavier, they build up their careers more slowly, focusing on developing skills and knowledge while rising at a steadier pace. Where Americans tend to spend five or fewer years with a single company (depending on their industry),[42] the French often remain

42 "Median Years of Tenure With Current Employer for Employed Wage and Salary Workers in the United States in 2024, by Industry," *Statista*, December 4, 2024, https://www.statista.com/statistics/1211900/us-employed-workers-median-years-tenure-industry/.

with an employer for at least twice that long.[43] Perhaps this is why French CEOs tend to stay in their jobs longer than leaders in other countries.[44] CEOs of French companies appear to be more resistant to constant removal, likely because they know the company and the position so well.[45]

Because the French rise up the career ladder more slowly, they can also focus on thoughtful spending decisions that match their current income and reduce longer-term financial pressure. Chetan, a friend of mine at Pitney Bowes, has embraced this philosophy in his own life. He recently invited me over to his place. Though he's become a real success at the company, I was surprised to see he had stayed in his original home, which was much less opulent than you'd expect of someone in his position.

When I asked him about this discrepancy, he told me that he'd bought his home based on his income at the time and locked in his mortgage when the rates were low. Instead of buying a new house with every promotion, he had paid the loan off early and was now financially secure for the rest of his life.

At some point, those wise decisions mean he won't even need his job anymore. Instead of needing a promotion to keep up with his expenses, he'll be able to work in any capacity he wants. He won't have to worry about saving enough for retirement or keeping his head above water when tougher financial times arrive. He can do what

---

43 Katharina Buchholz, "Where People Stick With Their Jobs," *Statista*, December 7, 2020, https://www.statista.com/chart/20571/average-time-spend-with-one-employer-in-selected-oecd-countries/.

44 Emily Douglas, "Which Nationality of CEOs Stay the Longest?" *HR Grapevine*, July 31, 2017, https://www.hrgrapevine.com/content/article/news-2017-07-31-which-nationality-of-ceos-stays-the-longest.

45 "2023 CEO Transitions in Europe," *SpencerStuart*, March 2024, https://www.spencerstuart.com/research-and-insight/2023-ceo-transitions-in-europe.

makes him happy and gives him purpose, safe in the knowledge he already has enough.

That kind of freedom is rare. To earn it, he's had to give up on some of the glitz and glam of flashier purchases. But I'd say the benefit is usually worth it.

## The Value of Expertise

Besides job retention and greater financial security, the slower path is often the better one for employers as well. When employees focus on developing deep expertise in their field, they experience greater job satisfaction, engagement, and a sense of purpose in their work. Research by the *Harvard Business Review* suggests that employees who have the opportunity to develop deep expertise are more likely to experience a sense of purpose and fulfillment in their work.[46] This can lead to higher-quality work, increased innovation, and a more committed workforce.

The reason for this is simple. Mastering a skill can be stressful at the time, but ultimately, it makes us happy.[47] And happy employees aren't as eager to leave. In contrast, those who focus on a careerist mindset that prioritizes promotion over all else usually feel lower levels of job satisfaction and engagement.[48]

---

46 Teresa M. Amabile and Steven J. Kramer., "The Power of Small Wins," *Harvard Business Review*, May 2011, https://hbr.org/2011/05/the-power-of-small-wins.

47 "No Pain, No Gain: Mastering a Skill Makes Us Stressed in the Moment, Happy Long Term," *Medical Xpress*, October 29, 2009, https://medicalxpress.com/news/2009-10-pain-gain-mastering-skill-stressed.html.

48 Amy Wrzesniewski and Jane E. Dutton, "Crafting a Job: Revisioning Employees as Active Crafters of Their Work," *Academy of Management Review* 26, no. 2 (2001): 179–201, https://positiveorgs.bus.umich.edu/wp-content/uploads/Crafting-a-Job_Revisioning-Employees.pdf.

All of which is to say, offering your people a slower path focused on developing all the skills related to their profession can actually improve engagement and retention. People will choose the slower path up if you make it more readily available.

And chances are, if you do provide that option, those who choose to stick around for the slow ride up will end up being your best people. William N. Thorndike Jr.'s *The Outsiders* is a perceptive book on leadership success for many reasons. None other than Warren Buffett recommends all CEOs read it. But one of the book's most interesting suggestions is that leaders who put aside all the glamor of their role and focus on their depth of understanding tend to be the most effective. The ones who forget about the limousines, put aside their egos, and earn their positions—those are your future leaders.

## Layering Your Knowledge

The path to expertise, whether for yourself or those you mentor, follows one of two fundamental approaches: You can either go deep, becoming a specialist in a narrow field, or go broad, developing knowledge across multiple domains.

Depth tends to cover a narrow, specific area of expertise. One of the most compelling examples of the depth approach comes from Bill Gates, whose legendary command of complex topics stems from a deliberate learning strategy. His ability to dive deep into specialized subjects and emerge with masterful understanding illustrates the power of focused knowledge acquisition. How does he have so much information at his fingertips?

He's answered this question before. He uses what's called the layering effect. Essentially, he layers knowledge on knowledge by building understanding through his reading habits. When he becomes interested in a certain topic—say, AI—he picks up a well-known book on the subject. That book will inevitably include citations and recommendations for other books, so he picks up one of those, which also has citations and recommendations. And so on. This process not only provides him with new information; it also cements key understandings in his mind as he goes because the same studies and concepts are reiterated across multiple texts.

It doesn't take that long to learn more about one specific topic than 95 percent of the people around you. If you keep the process up, before you know it, you'll become an expert.

This is, essentially, the same process by which an academic becomes an expert. Through classes, research, conferences, writing, and teaching, they learn new, updated information about their subject, all while core ideas become entrenched and nuanced with each new book or lecture.

Despite this process working so effectively, we rarely encourage it in most other areas of work. We don't ask our sales teams to read a book a month on a particular sales strategy, for instance. And most of us rarely read more than a single book on a topic, even when we're really interested.

In France, though, niche experts are extremely common. A company such as IBM has many experts like this. Pierre, whom I mentioned in the introduction, was the company's expert in allocation methodology. And this was by no means unique to IBM. In every French city, you could find experts who know how to repair a certain type of shoe better than anyone else and experts in a certain type of beading using certain types of material. They developed this expertise through a similar layering method—simply adding practice, experimentation, mentorship, and conversation to the tools to increase their knowledge.

I've experienced the power of this phenomenon in my own work. When I was tasked with converting a hardware company into a SaaS model, I read a lot about companies that had successfully done it before me. Netflix was the obvious example, so I started there. But steadily, I dove deeper and deeper, and I developed the more complex understanding of the process of an expert.

Again, though, finding some narrow subject you love, educating yourself, and continuing to dig until you have a deep understanding is only one way to gain expertise. The other is to layer your knowledge by breadth. This is the path Xavier took and the path my own career ended up taking as well. I didn't stay in one niche field and learn everything about it. Instead, I went into finance, where I learned pricing and balance sheets; then I went into sales, where I took the knowledge I already had and supplemented it with knowledge about sales techniques with various products.

At the end of six months in sales, I'd learned all the tricks of the sales trade. And because I knew all the financial tricks as well, I ended up the top seller for the department.

From there, I moved into strategy and did the same thing: I brought everything I'd learned in sales and finance into that field and combined it with the new knowledge I picked up in my new field. This broad layering is a great recipe for long-term training in leadership. Very often, senior leadership struggles because each person's experience is so narrow. They know finance and nothing else about the company. Mark Lockridge—one of the best CFOs I ever worked with—said one of the secrets of his success was that he'd been a general manager in sales as part of his career trajectory. Because he understood the sales experience, he had a deeper appreciation for process and employee needs across the whole company.

We live in a knowledge-based world, and neither of these paths is entirely right or wrong. The narrow path tends to lead to specialists, while the broader path tends to lead to leadership, but this isn't exclusively true. The only thing we can say for certain here is this: If you care about success in your field, the best way forward is to take the time to follow one of these paths.

You also don't have to explicitly make this decision immediately. Often, the best way to develop knowledge—either broadly or deeply—is to take the opportunities that come your way.

My former boss at Pitney Bowes, Marc Lautenbach, once taught me an incredible lesson about communication using an assignment. He asked me to write a strategy deck. I spent weeks on that project. After all that labor, my deck came out to forty well-polished, well-phrased pages. It was detailed, it was well written, and it was very impressive if I do say so myself.

Marc looked it over, and he agreed. But then he threw a curve ball my way: "Now, I want you to condense it down to ten pages."

It took a really long time to condense everything down. Every page seemed important, but after another epic struggle with the written word, I got it down to ten.

"This is fantastic," Marc told me at my next review. "Now get it down to one page."

After that round of edits, I had to get it down to a paragraph. Finally, he asked me to condense it down to one sentence.

The point of this exercise was to learn how to communicate the complex quickly. It's an important skill, and one I had to hone for Marc. But that kind of experience is far rarer if your focus is solely on the rush to progress. That assignment took months and a lot of effort. It didn't result in a promotion. Because I was looking to improve as much as to get promoted, I took full advantage of the lessons Marc offered me.

I found this activity so valuable that it's now a cornerstone exercise with all my mentees.

## Find What Makes You Unique

One of the real benefits of focusing on slowing down and developing yourself within your career is the opportunity to find what makes you distinct in what you do. The French have a term, *métier*, which technically just translates as a trade or profession, but there's nuance to the term. Métier emphasizes the importance of developing a high level of skill and expertise in a specific domain and connecting it to your purpose and the qualities that give the work meaning to you.

Essentially, you take whatever position you have, and you add one adjective that makes it unique to you. A plumber who loves Aristotle becomes the philosophical plumber—the person who chats about ethics while fixing your pipes. A clothing designer who loves delicious, rich food becomes the gourmand designer whose shop always smells like freshly baked bread, good cheese, and olive oil.

As you find your own way forward at your own pace, you should embrace the chance to personalize what you do, creating a unique version of your career. Being the accountant with a flair for marketing makes you more interesting than every other accountant at your company. It also improves your own enjoyment of the work and makes you more valuable to your employer. You combine qualities no one else does.

At IBM, I was the manager who demanded early evenings off for family time. I used to call lunch meetings with executives because I felt dinner meetings were harder on those with young families, particularly women. That priority set me apart, made me stand out, and helped me rise up the company ladder. These days, I'm the executive at Pitney Bowes with a financial lens and a passion for improving life–work balance for everyone on my team—yes, that means bringing everyone together with a little French flair. It's what makes me a unique leader across the whole company.

If you can find that métier and articulate it, you can improve your own perspective on your work, all while opening new opportunities for success.

## You Are in Control of Your Career

Many people feel like their lives and careers are out of their control. They think they have to accept whatever comes their way. But that is often an exaggeration. We have more power over what happens in our lives than we claim. And when you accept that fact, you can recognize that you can choose how quickly you move through life. In other words, taking your life and career along the scenic route is entirely your decision.

Bosses rarely force promotions on their people. If you want more experience in another area of business, often all it takes is putting your name out there for an opportunity. Once you open your eyes to the possibility, you may find there are more opportunities to layer your experience and knowledge than you first assumed. And no one is stopping you from finding the métier that will make your work more fulfilling and your position more valuable.

My daughter, Aliya, discovered this recently during her summer internship. She is in software engineering, and she worked for Pitney Bowes over break. At the start of that summer, the company told all the interns it was giving away $50 gift certificates to anyone who found out what lockers five different universities used. She could have ignored the offer, but what young adult can't use an extra $50?

So she contacted some friends, and she quickly discovered that while they were happy to help, they were puzzled by one thing: What was Pitney Bowes? They'd never heard of it.

This got Aliya thinking. Why not see this lack of awareness in the younger generation as an opportunity? Despite working in tech, she came up with a TikTok marketing campaign where Pitney Bowes made fun of the fact no one knew who they were. I suggested she take the idea straight to our marketing department, and they loved it. Suddenly, Aliya was spending part of her internship in a completely new area of the business, and she found out she really liked it.

Suddenly, she had found her own métier. She's not just any astrophysicist—she's the one with a talent for viral marketing.

These sorts of cross-pollination opportunities are all over the workplace. I regularly have projects that require input from multiple departments. I also make a point of having everyone in finance go on at least one sales call each quarter. This gives finance more perspective on how their work affects the rest of the company and our clients, but it also gives more of that broad experience that can be so valuable as a career progresses.

These same kinds of opportunities are present all around us all the time. If you enter every conversation with curiosity, you never know what you might learn. Instead of passing by the list of free classes in your town, go to one. Be open to seeing things differently—to new ideas, new knowledge, and new ways of doing things. That kind of active curiosity can open up new potential to enjoy life and reach your full potential, especially if you're willing to take the slower path to get there.

## Go Deep Across Your Life

All this talk of work is important, but we have to remember that part of our goal in life is to understand ourselves and our place in the world beyond the office. Who are we? What do we want? What are we trying to do here? These aren't questions you can answer through a deep dive into a particular coding language or by developing a broad understanding of hiring practices at your company.

But the same advice—taking the slower path—helps here too. Climbing the ladder quickly, we tend to define ourselves by what others need us to be, not who we naturally are. If we go more slowly, we can find ourselves and develop who we are as we go.

These abilities—layering our knowledge and finding our métier—can be used in other areas of our lives as well. We can layer our knowledge into our hobbies and find our métier in our family life. We can also recognize the importance of quality over quantity. Just like a slower rise allows us to catch our breath and adjust to a new income level instead of just constantly spending, we can also reevaluate our connection to *stuff* in general.

Life doesn't have to be about constant change, change, change. That change often creates extra stress without much reward. Slowing down and choosing to define ourselves—that's a powerful way to seize some control over our own lives and live it on our own terms.

## *La Vie Française in America*

Three ways to start living the French lifestyle today

1. Dig more deeply into the subject you named in the last chapter. Don't just stick with the podcast or the first book you read. Find one of their original sources and read that.
2. Before you make your next big purchase, take some time to consider whether you really need it. Is this purchase fulfilling a real need? Would that money be better spent or invested elsewhere? If that money could get you a little closer to long-term financial freedom, would that be a better use?
3. Figure out your unique brand. Are you a dentist with a passion for history? A philosophical marketer? What makes you *you*? Bring up the questions and your answers with three friends or coworkers to find out if they see you in the same light.

# CHAPTER 6

## Le Village

The French enjoy a good vacation more than most people, and that philosophy extends to how they schedule schooling. Instead of requiring students to go to class for months on end without a break, they divide most of the year into two-month segments: six weeks on, two weeks off. The exception to that schedule is August, of course, which most families take off, as well as July.

This year-round schooling approach helps reduce the risk of kids burning out. They're never that far away from another chance to catch their breath and enjoy being kids. It also reduces learning loss because those same children are never that far away from returning to the classroom.

But as every parent around the world knows, time off for the kids is not time off for the parents. Early on, the French year-round school schedule was brutal for me and Fayyaz. We both worked long hours, and Fayyaz's job required him to travel out of the country regularly.

We considered daycare options, but we felt guilty sending the kids anywhere but school. So, initially, we split the time between us, each taking a week off.

As you can imagine, within a few months, that proved completely unsustainable. Instead of spending vacation time on travel or relaxation, it was full-time stay-at-home parenting just to make sure Qaahir and Aliya weren't left alone for days on end.

This arrangement was particularly stressful for me because I was determined to do everything. I had vowed to myself that I would continue to have my career, but I had also vowed that I'd be the fun parent, the education parent, and the one who introduced my children to all kinds of new experiences. Each of those roles was a full-time job—in truth, more than a full-time job—and I didn't have the time, the energy, or the vacation days to pull it all off all the time.

After each week off, I'd come back to work more exhausted than before I left. You can imagine my mix of envy and amazement when I contrasted my situation with that of Annie, my friend at work. She had three children—ranging in age from five to twelve—and was having a fourth. Somehow, she seemed to handle it all so effortlessly. She spent time with the kids every evening, took relaxing vacations with the whole family every year, and made it to work on time, looking rested and focused.

"What's your secret?" I asked her desperately. "How can you have the energy to have four children? I'm barely holding on with just two."

I explained how Fayyaz and I were struggling with those school breaks, and she gave a gentle, compassionate laugh.

"You poor woman! No, no, no, I could not have one child on your schedule, let alone four! But that is not how you are meant to fill those days in France."

Annie told me about these places, *centres aérés*, essentially short outdoor camps that run during the school breaks. Also called *colonies de vacances*, these programs exist around the country specifically to keep children busy, safe, and engaged during those school breaks. For only about $100 a week, kids can run around, play, and learn outside for all the same hours they would normally be at school. Depending on which centre your kids go to, they might do artwork, go to museums, or learn horseback riding. Most French families break up those two weeks with one at a centre and the other with one set of grandparents or the other.

A week of care for Qaahir and Aliya each break would make a world of difference. We decided to give it a try. After sending the kids the first time, they came back so happy that we knew we'd made the right decision. We doubled down on the centre each break.

Finding a way to rely more on family proved a little harder. Obviously, neither Fayyaz nor I had any family in France—or anywhere on the continent. But eventually, we did find a way to include them in our plans, sending the kids back to Canada for longer breaks from time to time.

I remember the first time I sent Aliya to Vancouver to visit my parents. Before the flight, she was so nervous and upset. She didn't want to leave her mother. So, I came up with a little trick for her. I gave her a "bottle of hugs"—little paper hearts that each represented one hug from me. Anytime she missed me, she could pull one out.

Watching her walk into the terminal for her first solo flight, I worried whether that was enough to keep her from missing home. But just like the centre, once I let go a little, I discovered that bit of freedom and the new experience was exactly what she had been needing. She had such a good time in Vancouver that she never used any of those hearts. In fact, she gave the whole bottle to her grandparents when she headed back home.

You can only imagine my relief when she told me. From having to stretch myself in every direction, I suddenly had options to entertain, educate, and enrich my children's lives while I could work guilt-free. As they say, *Il faut tout un village*. It really does take a village.

## Take Away the Guilt Factor

America doesn't make it easy to work and have a family. It's the only wealthy nation without any paid maternity or paternity leave when a child is born.[49] The country also spends less than its peers on all manner of support for children.[50] The prevailing expectation in American culture demands that parents simultaneously maintain successful careers, manage pristine households, sustain healthy lifestyles, and provide their children with constant, devoted attention.

Women, in particular, get caught up in trying to make this overwhelming puzzle fit together, and this is all the harder during those long American summers when the kids are home. The two-week gaps were tough in France, but at least there was more vacation time to draw from, as well as the month of August we all had off together. In America, the breaks may be more infrequent, but they are very long and feel impossible to fill.

There are ways to make this schedule work and to find real life–work balance, but before we can consider any of the solutions out

---

49 Kendra Hurley, "The U.S. Leaves Parents on Their Own for a Reason," *The Atlantic*, June 15, 2022, https://www.theatlantic.com/family/archive/2022/06/us-paid-parental-leave-child-welfare-tax-credit/661276/.

50 Claire Cain Miller, "How Other Nations Pay for Child Care. The U.S. Is an Outlier." *The New York Times*, October 6, 2021, https://www.nytimes.com/2021/10/06/upshot/child-care-biden.html.

there, we have to start by removing the guilt factor from the equation. One of the main reasons I didn't look for childcare in Paris was a sense that relying on others to watch my children while I worked made me a bad mom. Like I said above, I felt I had to do it all: work, take care of the kids, and also cook and keep everything clean and tidy.

Getting it all done is impossible. We must give ourselves permission to share responsibilities and embrace support from others. We also have to give ourselves permission to set boundaries and priorities. Most of us have been trained to be accommodating. When someone falls behind or can't fulfill their responsibilities, we step in. But do someone else's work often enough or well enough, and it will eventually become yours. Everyone will assume you can just handle it.

Instead of holding others accountable and making sure any accommodation is temporary, we give our time away. This is bad for you, and ultimately, it's bad for those handing you the responsibility—whether it's a company, a spouse, or a friend. Handing more tasks to an already overburdened person is just going to lead to issues down the line in one area or another.

I always say that I don't want heroes in my department. Heroes are great—for one quarter. They'll step up and do everything, but that isn't sustainable or scalable. You don't want the same person stepping up all the time, and if you have that, eventually, they'll burn out, and all those responsibilities will have to be reassigned anyway.

In other words, we have to get more comfortable saying no to more. This was a key lesson former CEO of IBM, Lou Gerstner, taught me when I met him at a conference years ago. It was his policy to clear a couple of hours from his schedule each day for creative thinking because that was the most valuable use of his time. But to keep that time free, he had to set boundaries and say no to a lot of demands.

## It's OK to Step Away

To relieve our guilt, to set boundaries and say no, we have to accept that we don't have to be at the center of everything. This is difficult for parents and those in leadership. It's hard to put full trust in others to complete the project without our overview or to take care of our kids without us standing over their shoulders.

Americans are famous for their helicopter parenting, but French parents don't feel bad about sending their kids to a centre aéré. That time away from home is considered character building. Parents are doing their kids a favor by sending them away for a week! The children have fun, have some interesting experiences, and come home energized. That time away is valuable to them because they get to discover who they are on their own terms.

In the hyper-involved American version of parenting, our culture tells us that kids should never be out of sight and never on their own. Parents literally exhaust themselves trying to raise their children 24/7.[51] They micromanage routines and take an obsessive interest in their children's friendships, hobbies, and schoolwork. They track their sleep cycle and what they eat. This is not an exaggeration. My son once went on a playdate with an American friend. On the wall of his friend's house was the kid's daily schedule, with his time blocked out to the minute. Many parents these days start fretting about college applications before their children can walk.

This isn't good for our children, who need to build independence, or for ourselves, who need rest and a life of our own. Children are less free than they were in the past, under pressure not just to succeed academically but to meet their parents' expectations in terms of their

---

51 Rachel Minkin and Juliana Menasce Horowitz, "Parenting in America Today," *Pew Research Center*, January 24, 2023, https://www.pewresearch.org/social-trends/2023/01/24/parenting-in-america-today/.

social and emotional development. They have little privacy and little time to themselves, all while they're taught to fear the world, even though we live in a safer time.[52]

This has long-term consequences. Children who have been over-parented may struggle more with romantic relationships in adulthood.[53] It may also lead to higher levels of anxiety, poor coping skills, and lower self-esteem, among other things.[54]

In contrast, kids thrive when given more autonomy. Sharing the responsibility of childcare with others gives them new experiences. It's a chance for your kids to enjoy a changer d'air while also developing skills of self-reliance and coping with their emotions.

A similar dynamic exists in the workplace. Our teams can never develop if we always take the lead and do all the heavy lifting. They, too, need autonomy away from your ever-present attention.

In other words, we're doing no one any favors by putting this all on our own shoulders and refusing to step away. We need to accept our own limits and the value of letting others step up to take some of the burden.

## Build Your Support Structures

When you open yourself up to it, the support you need is more available than you assume. Once you get over the guilt of needing

---

52 Arthur C. Brooks, "Don't Teach Your Kids to Fear the World," *The Atlantic*, September 1, 2022, https://www.theatlantic.com/family/archive/2022/09/the-best-way-to-teach-kids-about-danger/671310/.

53 Chengfei Jiao et al., "Overparenting and Romantic Relationships in Emerging Adulthood: Roles of Relationship Efficacy and Parent–Child Relationship Quality," *Family Relations* 27, no. 5 (July 25, 2024): 3015–3030, https://doi.org/10.1111/fare.13070.

54 Draven Porter, "10 Troubling Signs of Overparenting and Its Consequences," *Marriage.com*, March 28, 2024, https://www.marriage.com/advice/parenting/overparenting/.

assistance, there are a lot of options for you. Often, the reason we don't receive this support is because we don't know who to ask and we don't know what we're asking for.

For that reason, the easiest way to reduce the load you're carrying is to start by inventorying that load. Make a list of all the things you have to do—professionally and personally—and break it down into what you absolutely have to do (whether you like it or not), what you like to do, and what you don't like doing.

For everything in that third category, consider your options. At home, if you don't like cooking, is there a service you could use or someone you could ask to help out? If you look for help, how many meals would you need each week? What kind of meals are they? At work, if you don't have to participate in a particular meeting, could you get someone who goes to share their notes?

Some solutions may be closer to home than you expect. When our kids were young, Fayyaz and I realized that we both had strengths and weaknesses as parents. He didn't love getting down on his knees and playing with the kids, but I absolutely did. At the same time, he loved cooking for them and keeping the house nice. So, we divided the work across our strengths. He did more of the housekeeping, and I did more of the playing.

It takes less energy to do what you like and what you're good at than going against the grain. At the same time, forcing yourself to do those tasks you find unpleasant makes them unpleasant for everyone. Kids know when you are phoning it in. They notice that you're staring at a screen instead of listening to their story or that every meal is cooked in the microwave. Dividing tasks with your partner can allow both of you to prioritize what you love and what you're good at—in marriage, housekeeping, and family.

You can do the same at work when delegating certain responsibilities. Everyone is great in certain areas of their work and less successful in others. Instead of trying to build up those weak muscles to lift every task, find someone to do the work who already has strength in that area.

Beyond your immediate family or team, you can also find more support than you might realize simply by making specific asks. The French are very straightforward about pawning their kids off on their grandparents. Usually, one set of grandparents (the ones who live farther away) take the kids during those extended breaks, and the other set (who live closer) take the kids on occasional weekends or evenings when the parents need a break.

Obviously, not all grandparents, either in France or America, are willing or able to take on that responsibility, but I'm confident that more would do so if simply asked. And again, this is not a dereliction of duty as a parent. It does your kids a lot of good to spend time with their relatives. There's immense value in giving them a sense of two (or more) homes with family who will love them and keep them safe. It's a chance to pass down family traditions to them that they might otherwise miss. And taking care of kids keeps grandparents young and the family close.

And these opportunities aren't limited to just grandparents. You can leverage your entire support structure. Siblings, cousins, aunts and uncles, friends—if any of them can help, ask. Aliya is planning to visit her cousins in Canada soon, and they're currently fighting over which house she'll stay in because they all want time with her. That's often the reaction people receive just for asking. Family and friends are more willing to help than you might assume.

When you ask for help, though, it's important to offer reciprocity. It's great if your parents will watch your kids for the weekend, but you shouldn't just drop them off and pick them up like it's a daycare. You have to spend time with your parents as well. They miss you too. If your sister cooks meals for you while your kids are young, you should offer to help pack if she moves. That's the nature of community and support.

My friend, Hilary, was always ready to watch our kids so Fayyaz and I could get some time together, but we did the same for her and her family. We took care of one another; we shared the burden, so no one was truly left to do it all alone.

Even if you leverage every relationship in life and at work, you'll never clear every unpleasant task off your list, but you can free yourself of more than you probably assume. All it may take is knowing what you're asking for and finding the courage to ask for it.

## Delegate and Share the Burden

For the rest of that list, there's another option: you can pay someone to do the work for you. In his book *Life Leverage*, Rob Moore recommends we should delegate tasks in life the same way we do at work. In business, if you could make more of an impact doing something else, you would hand your current responsibility off to someone else and focus on that more valuable project, right? We can use this same framework when considering all our obligations in life.

Do you enjoy mowing your lawn? Is it worth the hour or so it takes to keep it neat? Is there something else you'd rather do with that hour?

There are no right answers here. Maybe you do really look forward to that hour out in the sunshine. But if you'd rather spend that time with your spouse or your kids, or just taking a nice walk, it's worth the cost to pay someone else to tend to that responsibility.

The same is true of everything in your life. For instance, I have someone who comes in and cleans my house because I don't enjoy that activity. Cleaning would take too much of my free time, cutting into those Sundays I like to leave open. So, I delegate. I happen to like cooking, but if you don't—and if your spouse doesn't either—that's another easy responsibility you can hand to others. There are tons of services these days that will ship ready-made meals to your home. You can also use Uber Eats to bring healthy meals straight from the restaurant.

And we may not have colonies de vacances in America, but most towns have summer camps. The Boys & Girls Club runs all year and always has activities for kids. That's often the case at your local YMCA as well. These are affordable, well-run, safe places where your kids can go, have fun, and develop while giving you a little guilt-free time to work or take care of yourself.

If your town doesn't have these organizations, or if they're otherwise a poor fit for your family, you could consider sharing the responsibility of watching kids across several families. Reach out to a few other families and see if everyone would be interested in rotating weekends or days watching all the kids in the group.

While building social support systems and delegating tasks can significantly lighten our daily burden, there's one final pillar of security that can transform how confidently we navigate these choices: financial preparedness. Just as the French social system provides a safety net that allows families to make different choices, we can create our own security through thoughtful financial planning.

## Build Your Own Parachute

One final way to reduce the stress and responsibility on your shoulders is to create more financial support for yourself. One of the reasons French people stress less about work and childcare is because the French welfare state does more for them. The centres aérés are affordable on most budgets. They don't have enormous medical bills, and they receive generous unemployment and retirement benefits. America famously has a far more limited safety net. This leads to people working harder and longer, obsessing over their job security and income.

But this system has its benefits, too, if you know how to use them. The French are taxed at a far higher rate to cover all the costs of those systems. There's no reason that you can't take the extra income that comes home with you and put it toward savings that offer the same security.

I've always recommended to my kids that they put away 10 to 20 percent of what they make until they have at least an entire year's salary set aside. This is not your standard 401(k) investment. Instead, it's an emergency fund. That way, if and when those medical bills show up, you can pay them. If and when you lose your job, you won't struggle.

Crucially, this money is meant to be there just for emergencies. It isn't to splurge on a big vacation. Its purpose is mostly peace of mind. We live in a highly disruptive period. Who knows how AI will affect jobs or when the next recession will hit? Instead of staying up at night worrying (or worse, ignoring the risk until it hits you), you can create a parachute that will take care of you and your family no matter what happens.

With that parachute in place, it's a lot easier to make better decisions about your time and priorities. If you know you're financially secure, you can afford to say no to more responsibilities at work. If you know you'll be OK, you can feel more comfortable stretching to cover those lawn-care services or an extra couple weeks of summer camp.

More financial security makes it easier to take full advantage of the village, using its resources more wisely. And it also can give us more confidence in our own self-sufficiency.

---

## *La Vie Française in America*

**Four ways to start living the French lifestyle today**

1. Break down all work and life responsibilities into what you have to do, what you like to do, and what you'd rather not do.
2. Leverage the strong relationships in your life to help with those tasks you could hand off.
3. Pay for the services that could reduce your burden at home and work.
4. Create your parachute plan.

---

# CHAPTER 7

## Community and Connectivity

Moving abroad is often romanticized. Perhaps I'm guilty of doing so in this book. A new start in a new country full of new experiences: The very idea sounds like a vacation from boring, everyday life. And it can be all those things—but it can be a lonely process too.

While there's so much to enjoy once you get settled, when you actually arrive in a new place where you don't know anyone, it can be overwhelming and isolating. The busy boulevards with thousands streaming past under leafy chestnut trees feel more crowded than charming, with the set expressions upon every face a sign no connection is possible, let alone welcome.

Perhaps such impressions would have been less intimidating if not for the fact I had left such a warm, comfortable home in Toronto. There, I was surrounded by family and community on all sides. I had multiple cousins who were a five-minute drive away. Every weekend, we spent time in each other's homes. I also had a busy and full life with friends, colleagues, and gregarious neighbors. My problem back in Canada was finding time to be alone, not finding people to do things with.

Once in France, I went from an almost too-active social life to nothing. No family, no friends, no colleagues, and no obvious ways to change that. It's tough to forge new connections at the best of times, let alone in a new country and in your second language. It didn't help that we were living in remote Chantilly at the time (which was beautiful but hardly the place to find opportunities to meet a lot of new people) or that Fayyaz was constantly away on business. On those early business trips, I went days without talking to anyone.

With good reason, then, Fayyaz worried I might become depressed. In the state I was in, those gray Parisian skies and wet cobblestone streets could start looking more bleak than romantic pretty quickly. So, Fayyaz secretly began researching ways to support me and improve my mental health, and he read that pets are a great way to do that.

Without speaking to me about it, he bought me a friendly, excitable golden retriever puppy. It was an incredibly sweet gesture; there was just one, little problem: I had a fear of dogs.

Luckily, Avicenna was so charming that I fell in love with him despite myself. He was so loving and cuddly, I couldn't help getting over my fear. Fayyaz had been right: A dog was just what I needed. Avicenna was someone to talk to, and taking care of him gave me something to do on those long days alone.

Avicenna brought another unexpected benefit as well. Because I had never had a dog, I had to start getting out of my shell more just to get advice. First, I spoke to the woman who owned the apartment we were renting, because she had experience raising dogs. Then, more conversations started coming my way just because I had Avicenna with me.

As Avicenna was an energetic pup still working on getting trained, I had to take him out half a dozen times a day, walking in the beautiful forest next door to our apartment building. It was on those walks that I really became a part of my new community. The world over, there's no better way to start a conversation than to take your dog for a walk and run into another dog owner out on their own stroll. My neighbors, who had previously passed by without a word, seemed to almost see me for the first time once Avicenna was in the picture. The first time we met, I would get a nod. The next time, we might say bonjour to one another. By the third or fourth time, though, some of them would hazard a bit of real conversation. And a few took that conversation even further.

On one walk in particular, Avicenna led to a wonderful friendship. We were out in the forest by our apartment building, and I was working on training Avicenna without his leash. I'd let him wander off a little way and then call him back. I was getting some mixed results.

"No, no, no," I heard behind me. Glancing over my shoulder, I saw my neighbor, Louis, who lived on the first floor of our building. He was older, with a gentle look about him. In this case, he was offering me some gentle advice. He'd been standing there listening for a bit, and he had some tips on my training technique.

"You have to correct the dog's name," he told me. "A dog's name should be one—or at maximum two—syllables. Yours is too long. You should rename him something like Descartes or Voltaire."

My pride a little bruised, I called out, "Avi," which the dog did not respond to at all. I then used his full name once more, "Here, Avicenna!" And this time, he came right away.

"I guess he's a smart dog," I shrugged.

But that little scrap of conversation was enough to intrigue my neighbor. "Where did you get this name for the dog?"

I explained that, in a way, I had already taken his advice. He'd named two French philosophers, and Avicenna—sometimes written Ibn Sina—was a famous Muslim philosopher from the eleventh century.

"Very interesting," he nodded. A short time later, we said goodbye. I didn't see him for a couple of weeks, but when we were next out with our dogs together, he approached me without hesitation. This time, he didn't have advice; he had questions.

"You must tell me about Ibn Sina's metaphysics. His theology is quite interesting, but I don't feel I quite grasp everything."

I stood there, shocked. Instead of just forgetting our little conversation, my neighbor had gone out and researched Ibn Sina. He'd been reading about the philosopher ever since, and he was trying to place Ibn Sina's ideas into his understanding of the Western philosophical canon.

I had to sheepishly admit that I really didn't know that much about Avicenna beyond his reputation, nor much about philosophy in general. But I followed his lead and went out a few days later to get an introductory book on major philosophers so we could keep the conversation going.

These little chats bloomed into a wonderful friendship. And his friendship was the true turning point that helped me settle into my new home. My neighbor helped me improve my French. He told me the fastest ways to get into Paris and which butcher and *fromager* were the best in the area. Over time, he introduced me to all our neighbors. He'd been in his apartment for twenty-five years, so he knew everyone. Because these introductions came with a reference, it made it easier to build real relationships.

Our friendship wasn't all one-sided either. When he needed to get to the hospital from time to time, he knocked on my door. He knew I was always there for him.

Thanks to him, I made connections and started feeling more positive, more welcome, and more comfortable. France didn't feel like Toronto, but for the first time, it felt like a place I could belong and be happy.

My journey from isolation to community in France taught me something fundamental about human nature and the way we're meant to live. It highlighted the profound difference between simply residing somewhere and truly belonging to a place.

## La Vie de Quartier

Human beings are meant to live in small communities where we know everyone, trust everyone, and share in all responsibilities. As I alluded to in the last chapter, one of the reasons modern life feels so overwhelming is that we do things alone that we evolved to do together. Our ancestors shared the burden of work, gathering food, childcare, and emotional support across their whole community.[55] We are most comfortable in an environment that best replicates those circumstances.

That's why it was so pleasant to become an active part of my quartier, or neighborhood, in France. Seeing the same people who all know you and are willing to provide a helping hand every so often makes a place feel like you belong. In France, I spoke to the same baker and the same fruit seller every day. I had a relationship with almost everyone I saw on the street.

These connections had real, practical value. One time, when my fruit seller found out from a neighbor that I was sick, he came by and left my regular order at the door on his way home. A small kindness,

55 "Human Characteristics: Social Life," *Smithsonian National Museum of Natural History*, January 3, 2024, https://humanorigins.si.edu/human-characteristics/social-life.

but it was one that meant he thought about me. Those small signs of support can mean the world when you're unwell.

I know it's hard to believe such communities still exist because most Americans generally feel isolated, even from their neighbors. Most Americans don't really know their neighbors, let alone feel like those neighbors provide a community.[56] At most, we wave and smile at one another or manage to say hello as we pass by. As a society, we're increasingly shrinking into our homes, meeting fewer people, making fewer connections, and having fewer romantic encounters.[57] We're simply living lonelier lives with fewer meaningful relationships.

Not only are we missing the kind of support I discussed in the last chapter when it comes to raising a family or reducing the burden we're carrying, but we aren't getting the emotional and social support we need as human beings. This support makes us feel good and like we belong somewhere, and that has profound effects on our health. People who feel connected to their community are healthier. They sleep better. They engage in more physical activity and eat better. In contrast, a lack of social connection can increase the risks of dementia, depression, heart attack, and stroke.[58]

Lacking a sense of community is literally killing us.

On some level, we know this. Many of the most popular shows of all time—*Friends*, *Seinfeld*, *Frasier*, *The Office*—are about close friends who get into fun situations in their community. Despite these shows being decades old at this point, they remain popular across all

56 Carly Mallenbaum, "It's Good for Your Health: Be a Better Neighbor," *Axios*, August 2, 2023, https://www.axios.com/2023/08/03/how-to-good-neighbor-mental-health.

57 Anton Cebalo, "Is America Suffering a 'Social Recession'?" *The Guardian*, January 2, 2023, https://www.theguardian.com/commentisfree/2023/jan/02/america-social-recession-less-friends-sex-mental-health.

58 "Social Connection," *U.S. Centers for Disease Control and Prevention*, May 15, 2024, https://www.cdc.gov/social-connectedness/about/.

age groups because we crave this kind of social interaction in our lives. And when we can't get it in person, we seek it out on screen.[59]

But again, we don't have to go to Netflix for these kinds of relationships. Those strong, close communities aren't works of fiction or a matter of history. They exist all over France. And they exist in America too. If you prioritize personal relationships with people in your community, it can be easier than you think to create this same environment in your own quartier.

## Social Connection Is Closer Than You Think

A lot of the social connections we crave are right in front of us; we just don't think to take advantage of them. It isn't so rare even today to hear about neighborhood Fourth of July cookouts, summer block parties, or community gardens. It only feels so far away because we've forgotten how to build these connections ourselves.

When I moved back to the US, I had the same issue I had when moving to France. I was in Connecticut, far from family and friends in Canada and Paris. Fayyaz was still working from France, and once again, I had no easy way to integrate myself into my community.

Luckily, I'd learned from my previous experience. I decided this time I wasn't going to wait for someone to approach me; I'd take the lead in building those relationships. Whenever I ran into one of my new neighbors, I made a point of introducing myself. I know being the first to engage can feel intimidating—it did for me when I was first in France—but I've witnessed firsthand how easy this is once you try.

---

59 Chris Melore, "Survey Ranks 20 Best TV Shows of All Time," *FOX59*, January 31, 2022, https://fox59.com/news/entertainment/survey-ranks-20-best-tv-shows-of-all-time/.

After all, the worst thing your neighbor can do is refuse to reciprocate your friendliness. And I've found that almost never happens anyway.

In fact, their reaction is often to reciprocate your offer of friendship.

This was certainly the case with my neighbor Andrew. The person who lived in our house before us did not get along with him. I was advised to stay well away from him. But I wasn't going to let their impression determine how I felt about my neighbor. So, when an opportunity presented itself to broach an introduction, I made a point of taking full advantage of it.

It all started with a mailbox. I wanted to move mine a couple of feet over from its previous location. Technically, I was still placing it on my property, but it was close enough that I felt I should ask Andrew what he thought. After registering surprise I'd even ask and quickly giving permission, we changed topics and dove into a real conversation.

We discovered immediately that we had a lot in common. It turned out Andrew was Polish, and we had a great chat about what we missed in Europe and what we liked better in America. We talked about Helena (his wife) and her love of Cadbury—she'd spent a lot of time in England and fell in love with the chocolate there—and how difficult it could be to find Cadbury Fruit & Nut or Dairy Milk around here.

From this one conversation, a whole friendship blossomed. A couple of months later, Andrew even fixed my house without me asking. He'd mentioned a few times offhand that the vents on the side of my house were deteriorating. They were plastic and hadn't been replaced in years.

"You should really take care of that," he'd warned. "Otherwise, you'll end up having a real problem."

I believed what he said, but the task just got away from me. I'd called the developer, and he couldn't fit me in on short notice. So it just kept getting put off.

One day, coming home from work, I saw that Andrew had pulled a ladder out and was fiddling around near my roof. He'd started repairing the vents for me. When I asked why he was repairing *my* house after a long day of work, he said, "I'm going to do this for you because I'm worried about you."

He refused to take anything for his efforts except the cost of materials for his work.

Fayyaz and I returned the favor later. On Fayyaz's way back from France, I had him pick up some Cadbury Fruit & Nut for Helena. Just like that, we'd become the sort of friends who do those little kindnesses for each other, just like the friends I'd made in France.

Even now, I'm still continuing my project to build more relationships in my neighborhood. I recently planned a get-together with all my neighbors while Fayyaz was in town. It was nothing special, just a chance to stop in, have some coffee and fresh croissants, and enjoy a little neighborly conversation.

No one else on my street would have instinctively thought to do this, but so what? All it took to add a little quartier charm to this area was the decision to bring some French culture to the neighborhood in the same way I brought those pastries from our local bakery, Raphaël's. That little bit of effort to reach out and offer friendship was all it took to start building a real community.

## Relearning the Lost Art of Conversation

Part of the reason taking the first step feels so intimidating is that we aren't used to walking up and starting conversations anymore. We've become so used to living on screens that we've lost the ability to initiate simple, straightforward interactions that allow communities to grow. Often, the hardest part of establishing stronger ties with those around you is finding a way to broach the subject. There's so much inertia that you have to push through that it feels like breaking through a barrier.

The only way forward is to recognize that this is the work you have to do in order to make a connection. No one else is going to do it for you.

It also doesn't have to be painful. Sometimes, all it takes is creating space for a conversation to happen. In France, whenever you go into a boutique, they always say bonjour and au revoir when you leave. Unlike the pushier American stores, where employees basically follow you around, they otherwise leave you alone. But those simple expressions are valuable because they communicate that there's room for more interaction if you need it. It says that you are free to ask questions and make conversation.

You can leave that opening for everyone. A simple hello to your neighbors, a quick conversation about the weather or an upcoming event, and you've offered an invitation for a deeper relationship.

Whether you're extending or accepting that invitation, though, be sure to make the effort to actually go deeper at some point. It's fine to start out talking about housing prices in the area or the new pizza place that opened down the road, but eventually, you want to seek out some shared interest or a common thread that ties you together. Whether it's Cadbury chocolate, golfing on Sundays, gardening, kids, or philosophers, these are the things that allow for real connection.

To find these shared interests, you have to do more than just leave an opening for conversation; you have to engage in it with real curiosity. Don't just focus on yourself and what's in your head. Approach others with a desire to listen and learn about someone else. My neighbor in France initiated our friendship because he was interested in the philosopher my dog was named after. I connected with Andrew because I was interested in his life in Poland and what he missed most about Europe.

Maybe that conversation about the new local pizza place can unearth a shared love of Italy or a shared passion for finding good, local restaurants with a unique menu. Maybe golf starts a conversation about working out in middle age or going on hiking trips.

Showing this kind of curiosity and shared openness is a life skill well worth developing. Once you sharpen it, you can discover unending threads you can weave into a community.

## Creating Space for Connection at Work

Sometimes, when seeking to build new connections, all you're missing is an opportunity. Maybe that opportunity comes in the form of offering some assistance. Relationships are built on taking care of one another, and you can take the lead here, too. Help a neighbor carry in their groceries or ask if they need someone to water their garden while they're on vacation. If they need a plumber, recommend the one you trust. These little offerings of support are the raw materials that bridge the gap between strangers and friends.

Alternatively, maybe all you need is a chance to sit down together in the same place for a little while. This is often the best way to build relationships at work. My daughter, Aliya, was recently working as an intern at Pitney Bowes. She went into the office a few times each week, and as I mentioned in chapter 5, this turned into a really impactful summer for her. She found a new interest in marketing. But there was one thing that she felt dampened the experience. She liked her boss and the people on the team she was working with, but she didn't really know anyone. Every relationship was strictly professional. She didn't really feel she had any peers she could connect with.

It was seven weeks before she realized there were several other interns on her floor. For nearly two months, she'd been no more than ten feet from someone going through the exact same experience as her without even knowing it, but due to the hybrid nature of the role, they had never been introduced.

It would have taken no effort at all to set aside one lunch a week for the interns to eat together and get to know one another. Just putting people going through the same experience in the same room often builds a community without any further effort. Many of us have experienced this in college. We can make some of our best friends just by living on the same floor in dorms during freshman year. Businesses may not be in the habit of getting new employees to room together, but a little shared time to compare experiences can help create deeper ties with colleagues and the company overall.

Such opportunities not only give people the opportunity to build community; they also have knock-on benefits for the company itself. Creating such communal ties often encourages people to stay longer with the company. It also allows management to find out who the future leaders of the organization might be. Look at who ends up organizing lunch orders and topics of conversation, and you probably have a person who could run a department in a few years.

It often takes very little work to create these opportunities for your team. In the onboarding process, I always give every new person a "buddy"—someone one or two layers up who has been with us for a while and knows all the unwritten rules. They can show the new person around, introduce them to everyone they need to meet, answer questions, and give them insight into the best places to get lunch nearby. It's these sorts of experiences that really build company culture and help someone integrate into a company immediately.

I don't just delegate these relationships either. I step in myself. When a new hire moves into town, I always share my real estate agent and explain the ins and outs of home buying in this area. It helps people settle in when you provide them with a skeletal network of support. They feel more secure, safer, and at home. At the same time, it communicates that I'm someone they can go to for advice and assistance when they need it.

Finally, I think there's a lot of value in building up the philanthropic arm of your company. Beyond the general good that such efforts can do, you really create the potential for people to get together outside work, do something together that isn't work related, and bond over that experience.

Of course, the only way any of these opportunities create connection and community is if people actually take advantage of them. If you are the one being offered a weekly lunch with team members, a "buddy" to show you the ropes, or a chance to do some volunteer work, take that opportunity with both hands.

I don't say yes to every volunteer opportunity, but if I feel I can make a difference in an area that matters to me, then I really throw myself into that work. It allows me to do some good in the world. But it also allows me to get to know people who share the same beliefs and concerns that I do. And what better start could you have for a community?

## Attention and Patience

I don't want to give the impression that the French are so open that it's easy to become fast friends and integrate into a community. If anything, the French often make this harder on people than Americans. When you walk around France, you'll notice almost immediately that no one smiles at you—particularly in Paris. Unlike Americans who smile almost reflexively, nod, and make eye contact with almost everyone, the French are very reticent about encouraging conversation and connection. It isn't that they aren't friendly; it's just a societal rule to be a bit more reserved with strangers. If you want to make a connection, you really do have to initiate—and you really have to stick with it.

Even leading with a friendly smile and a bit of conversation often produces the smallest of openings. It's generally a very slow thaw with French people. It takes a lot of time for them to truly open up to someone. I don't know how many times I invited my neighbors to come over to my place without any reciprocation. They would show up for a bit, but it took them almost fifteen years before one of them invited *me*.

Once I was in with someone in France, though, I was essentially family. I was invited to everything. They would do anything for me. The line between real friendship and acquaintance was very clear.

In a way, this is more honest than the American experience. The French are upfront about their real feelings. No matter the culture, it usually takes a long time to get close to someone. The French are just honest about this fact. In contrast, Americans and Canadians are famously open and friendly, but often only willing to go skin deep in a relationship. It's easier to walk up and start a conversation here, but the relationship often stagnates there. The same invisible wall goes up that keeps the relationship at a superficial level, but we're unwilling to be honest and straightforward about that.

Wherever you are, and however the person you're talking to presents themselves, the same challenge is before you. If you can push through that invisible wall, there is a real relationship available. I suspect it takes the same amount of time to break that wall down in America that it does in France.

We can dismantle that wall stone by stone through curiosity and openness. And to do that in the modern world requires two additional qualities that we've all allowed to erode in recent decades: patience and attention.

To truly be curious, we have to be willing to leave our phones and our responsibilities behind for a little bit. We may all have become accustomed to it now, but checking email or social media in the middle of a conversation isn't a natural way to communicate. In fact, it tells our conversation partner that we lack a genuine interest in what they're saying. In that fragile period between friendly conversation and real friendship, that can be enough to throw things off course.

I'm not blameless here. There are times that my son has had to physically reach over and close my laptop because my attention was drifting during lunch. My daughter Aliya has been known to pause a conversation until I was willing to stop texting and put my phone down.

For that reason, if finding or building a community is important to you, I recommend setting boundaries and being very disciplined with screens. In fact, if you are going out into your neighborhood or to an event, I think you should leave your phone behind. Don't let it even be a temptation.

It may feel like you have to answer a text right now, that an email can't wait, or that you really need to follow a story on social media, but this is almost always not the case. All of those things will still be there after you finish a conversation, attend a book club, or sit down for lunch with a colleague.

Even if you feel much of your community exists in an online format today, trust me, those digital connections are rarely as strong as those you create in the real world.

This is what we should really be talking about when we discuss quality time. So often, businesspeople use this expression to suggest they can cram all the important events in their children's lives into the limited time they assign to their families. That meaning never sat well with me because it suggests you can squeeze life into short little bursts between all the work you are committed to.

But that's not how life works. Those big events don't happen on your timetable. You can't pencil them into your calendar. Real quality time is about being present and paying attention so you are there and aware when the important moments happen. The big moments happen for an instant and then pass, and if you aren't available and you aren't paying attention, you'll miss them.

My neighbor, Mercier, once said to me on this subject, "The thing Americans don't understand is that you have to put in a lot of time because the quality time erupts at unexpected moments."

That's true when raising kids, and it's true when building connections with people around you. The quality conversation that can unlock a new friendship or a real sense you belong won't happen on a schedule, and if you're on your phone or thinking about work when it does arrive, you'll miss it.

This is one of the real secrets of French charm. The French are not innately more charming than Americans or Canadians. Instead, we mistake their direct attention and active listening for charm. The truth is, we feel flattered because someone is willing to pay so much attention to us, even if just for a moment.

Imagine how much stronger your own relationships would be if you granted that kind of attention to the people around you.

## *La Vie Française in America*

Three ways to start living the French lifestyle today

1. Pick one neighbor (whether an office neighbor or someone on your block) whom you regularly see around. Take a step to start a conversation. If that feels too intimidating, start with a smile and build up from there. Attempt three or four of these a year and see where these conversations take you.
2. Turn on the French charm. Choose three one-on-one conversations this week and give each your undivided attention. For thirty to sixty minutes, focus entirely on the other person. Try to make one conversation work related, one family related, and one with a friend. Keep this up for six months and journal on the impact this has on your relationships.
3. Find a community activity where you can volunteer. Read to kids at your library. Volunteer at The Salvation Army. Build a home with Habitat for Humanity. Create the social structure you wish to be a part of.

# CHAPTER 8

## Conversation Authentique

At the café, conversation is always boisterous. Whether discussing the day ahead over brioche and espresso, commenting on the quality of cassoulet at lunch, or engaging in a little after-business gossip while cutting into boeuf bourguignon, chatter always flows even more than the wine and is louder than the clinking of dozens of utensils on porcelain.

Along with all the pleasant topics covered in these charming, noisy tête-à-têtes, though, you'll also hear something unexpected to American ears most afternoons: arguments. The French are famous for their temper, and it's on full display at any restaurant.

To the French, a public airing of strong views isn't a sign of a dysfunctional relationship. In fact, it's the opposite. The French love to argue because they love to discuss their feelings and resolve disputes. They don't swallow their opinions as easily as they swallow foie gras. If they think you are making a mistake in your love life, they will tell you so. If they disagree with the direction a project is taking—they'll make sure you know it, whether in the office or over a meal.

I couldn't possibly count the number of times I saw couples launch into an argument in front of their friends out in public. While in America or Canada, we'd go pale at even the hint of a raised, frustrated voice, but this was more than just accepted behavior in Paris—it was encouraged. The friends sitting alongside the couple were often invited into the conversation to give their own views on the matter under dispute.

Like most people brought up in North America, in my early days in Paris, I took this behavior the wrong way. When I first started work at IBM, I spoke French to everyone. My French at the time was competent and fluent but far from perfect. I was comfortable speaking to my neighbors in French, but some of my colleagues took to correcting my mistakes. If I chose the wrong word or conjugated a rare verb incorrectly, they'd catch it and tell me about it.

I assumed this was done out of some sense of offense. Perhaps they felt I was butchering their language or else wanted to signal I should just give up and speak English. After all, they all spoke that language perfectly. So that's what I did. From then on, I engaged with everyone at IBM in English.

Years later, my previous boss, Didier, casually mentioned in conversation that it was such a shame I'd switched to English.

"You were making such progress," he told me.

By then, I knew the French well enough to guess my error. I'd taken their forthright corrections all wrong. My colleagues were being direct with me because they respected and liked me. They meant not to insult me but to help me improve. They cared enough to correct my mistakes. I just didn't know how to take the criticism.

## The French Correction

Americans and Canadians really struggle to be direct and honest with one another at times. We're so famously upbeat and positive that we shy away from any comment that might be perceived as critical. If you had to describe a stereotypical American comment, it'd probably be something like, "You're so amazing!" A stereotypical French comment, on the other hand, would probably involve a slight frown, a shrug, and something along the lines of "*C'est pas mal*"—essentially, "Eh, not bad." The meaning of that expression is clear: There's obviously room for improvement. Things could be better.

On a certain level, the American attitude is more pleasant to encounter on a day-to-day level, where we spend most of our conversation time engaging in shallow, friendly chitchat. But it comes at a cost. Criticism is a valuable part of communication. If we cut it out of our conversation, we increase the likelihood we'll make more—and more significant—mistakes.

According to Harvard Business School professor Michael Beer, one of the two main reasons managers fail is because the information they need from lower in the organization's hierarchy never gets to them.[60] People just aren't communicating criticism up the chain, and it costs leaders their jobs.

That isn't just a tragedy for the individual; it suggests that entire companies are being run poorly due to limited information flow up

60 Roger Trapp, "Why a Frank Conversation Could Be the Key to Transformation," *Forbes*, January 30, 2020, https://www.forbes.com/sites/rogertrapp/2020/01/30/why-a-frank-conversation-could-be-the-key-to-transformation/.

and down the organization. Longer term, that situation puts everyone's jobs at risk.

Conversely, more honest, direct conversation can improve individual relationships and entire organizations, increasing trust and creating a culture of learning and sharing ideas. Creating the space for diverse opinions to be voiced leads to better decision-making across the board. Perhaps as many as two-thirds of all business decisions are more effective when diverse feedback is included.[61]

At the same time, direct honesty is part of prosocial behavior that improves self-esteem, provides meaning in life, and tends to lead to better social benefits.[62] Honest communication may even improve our health. Where honesty has been tied to lower stress, "decreased cellular aging," and overall well-being, dishonesty raises blood pressure, heart rate, and levels of cortisol.[63] Avoiding direct, honest conversation, then, is bad for everyone on every level.

Importantly, we're talking about constructive criticism aimed at improving individuals and ideas. This isn't criticism for its own sake or the kind of brutal honesty designed to make someone look or feel bad.

Constructive criticism is all about encountering new perspectives that can push us forward. I recently watched a video of a father trying to fold a stroller so he could put it into the car. For three solid minutes, he wrestled with this thing. He tried pushing on it. He tried leaning on it. He flipped it over. He pulled the seat out

---

61 Kate Stone, "Diversity of Opinions: How to Be Inclusive of Ideas in the Workplace," *Diversio*, January 26, 2024, https://diversio.com/diversity-of-opinions/.

62 Van Doesum et al., "Social Mindfulness: Prosocial the Active Way," *The Journal of Positive Psychology* 15, no. 2 (February 18, 2019): 183–93, https://doi.org/10.1080/17439760.2019.1579352.

63 Leanne ten Brinke et al., "The Physiology of (Dis)Honesty: Does It Impact Health?" *Current Opinion in Psychology* 6 (December 2015): 177–182, https://doi.org/10.1016/j.copsyc.2015.08.004.

and put it back on. On and on he went. Eventually, two other men joined him to pull and push and wrestle with the contraption. In the final seconds of the video, a woman showed up. She walked over, placed a single hand on the stroller handle, calmly pressed a button, and instantly folded it.

It's a very amusing video, but there's a real lesson there. We need other perspectives in our work and our lives—diverse perspectives. And we're only going to encounter them if we leave ourselves open to frank, honest discussions.

## Meetings Should Be Noisy

So why don't we all just become straightforward conversationalists like the French? Mostly because this kind of communication is more difficult to master than it might seem. Most of us have become very comfortable with avoiding the direct truth in conversation. One study even found that 60 percent of people lie once every ten minutes.[64] Perhaps that's an exaggeration, but another study found that the average individual lies at least once or twice a day.[65]

We do this because we're convinced that we're making life easier—for ourselves and for those we speak to. To begin to change our behavior, we have to shift this perspective. As the Booth School of Business at the University of Chicago found, in reality, avoiding tough conversations is actually making life harder for us. In fact, telling the

64 University of Massachusetts Amherst, "UMass Researcher Finds Most People Lie in Everyday Conversation," *EurekAlert!*, June 10, 2002, https://www.eurekalert.org/news-releases/534347.

65 Jeff Hancock, "The Future of Lying," TED Talk, Manitoba, MB, September 2012, 18 min., 14 sec., https://www.ted.com/talks/jeff_hancock_the_future_of_lying.

truth is less painful than we expect and often offers more opportunities for connection and improvement over time.[66]

To overcome our natural resistance to direct and honest conversation, we have to create the circumstances that encourage such openness. We have to create structures and behaviors that encourage people to speak up. A French boardroom is a noisy place—in large part because everyone feels they have a right to share their perspective on the big topics under debate. Passions can run high, and voices can rise, but everyone knows it's in service of getting the best ideas out there.

In contrast, I've sat in many quiet meetings in America where all the real discussion has been done before the meeting itself. In executive circles, no one wants anyone to look bad, and no one wants to make their colleagues look bad. They fear that bringing up tough questions or sharing criticism of an idea will cause harm if done in front of the company's leadership. So, they have all their discussions beforehand, making meetings into cheerleading sessions with everyone on the same page.

Again, on the surface, this is a nicer way to hold meetings—but it's also a waste of everyone's time. If ideas aren't being contested in front of those who have to make the ultimate decision, those leaders aren't seeing all the possible solutions or knock-on consequences of their preferred choice. They also miss out on the *why* behind the decision. If the key individuals who made this call left the organization, it would be difficult to ever understand the logic that had led to that point.

---

66 Sandra M. Jones, "People Can Afford to Be More Honest Than They Think," *The University of Chicago*, September 21, 2018, https://news.uchicago.edu/story/people-can-afford-be-more-honest-they-think.

Recently, my team was debating how we should go about upgrading our customer relationship management (CRM) and enterprise resource planning (ERP) systems. Some of my team wanted to start with a new ERP system so we could tackle internal processes. Then, we could turn to CRM and external customer relationships. Others wanted to go the opposite direction, implementing a new CRM before taking on the thornier process questions that would come with a new ERP.

Many teams would have hashed out this discussion with leadership well out of earshot and then presented a single solution to the decision-maker at the top. I don't allow my team to behave that way—because that kind of process leaves me exposed to huge blind spots. In this case, thanks to our vigorous discussions, we all discovered that we had to make a decision on both systems at the same time because they share the same data. That was a huge potential liability that only surfaced because we talked the ideas out.

Similarly, our team conversations also recently unearthed a major inefficiency in our contracts. For decades, all costs have been placed on a single contract for clients. This included SaaS apps and hardware leases. This made sense back when the decision was first made because contracts were all physical documents. No one wanted to keep track of half a dozen contracts to separate out costs. These days, with everything digital, no one cares one way or the other.

If my team only made decisions within their silos, that process would have remained in place forever. Instead, through conversation, we were able to break down the reasoning behind the decision, and the potential knock-on complications for billing, legal, and procurement, and find our way to the best solution.

In both those conversations, there was clear disagreement in the meeting. Different perspectives were raised, and the discussion was a noisy affair. But in both cases, we reached the best possible decisions—and the noise helped us get there.

## Creating Room for French Discussion

In order for these types of open, authentic conversations to happen in American-style business meetings, you have to combine two ingredients: time and a culture that encourages an honest sharing of opinions. On the former point, I consistently prioritize making myself available to members of my team at all levels of authority. For the type of decisions I mentioned above, I reserve time for a biweekly "decision cadence" meeting—which I'll describe further in a moment. At the same time, though, I also run a town hall once a month and spend a lot of time in smaller groups where I try to connect with employees on a more personal, intimate level.

These meetings are an opportunity to explain why the company is doing what it's doing. Why are we pursuing this strategy over another? Why did we cut certain jobs in one department, and how can people feel secure they won't be next? I've found that ninety-nine times out of a hundred, once you explain yourself, the team will understand, and they will be 100 percent behind you.

The mistake many make is simply failing to create the space for open communication. This lack of dialogue leaves people no other choice than to come up with their own explanations for what they see happening. It's a bad policy that can create a lot of misunderstanding, and it also deprives you of some of the best advice available.

Some time ago, Diane, a woman who'd been with the company for thirty years, was on the line for one of these calls. At the end of the meeting, I opened things up to the whole field and set a pointed prompt: If you guys think we're doing something that basically means we're just giving away money—and if you think that we wouldn't lose clients by changing that policy—tell me about it.

When it was her turn, Diane floored me by revealing that we had had a policy on the books for more than a decade that offered a 5 percent discount to government clients just for running their plan through the web. Why, she asked, were we still offering this reduced price?

After the call, I did some digging—and she was absolutely right. The company had come up with the policy about twelve years earlier when there was a real push to move all our business accounts online. Back then, there were still a lot of holdouts—suspicious clients who weren't sure about the move. So, the company had offered them a little extra motivation.

Twelve years later, though, almost every account was online. Yet we were still giving away a discount. I got some pushback when I began the process of canceling this policy—with some insisting we'd lose a number of upset clients or, at the very least, that our call center would be overrun with complaints—but I had faith that Diane was onto something.

Once we finally implemented the policy, the results were far from the doom and gloom some had predicted. We didn't lose a ton of clients or even a few. In fact, we didn't lose any. And we only received one single complaint—which we quickly resolved by continuing their individual discount.

That action alone was worth $1 million in profit a year.

The situation made such a huge impression on me that I came to call Diane my million-dollar woman. What surprised me most in this situation, though, was her response when I shared the news. I was grateful she'd saved us a million dollars, but she was grateful in turn because she'd never been recognized like that before. No one had taken the time to hear her ideas or reward her for her insights.

In other words, this was only possible because I'd set time aside and created a structure that provided everyone with the space to open up, share honest opinions, and be listened to respectfully.

These same features can improve your personal interactions. If, like the French, you can find the time and create an understanding that encourages more honest discussions, a lot of those lingering issues that tie up friendships, romantic, and family relationships can be surprisingly easy to unknot. And if you're willing to allow some outside, friendly perspective by sharing those issues with others you trust, you may be surprised how much more clearly you can see all the perspectives involved in the disagreement.

The French are fond of regular dinner parties, but at these often-monthly events, they try to add some variety. It's so easy to fall into groupthink—even when just conversing with two or three people. To counter this, the French will invite around eight guests to one of these parties. But each month, four of those guests will change.

This keeps things fresh and the conversation and perspectives new. When family or friends are going through a turbulent moment, these parties can function as a sort of group therapy, with those new opinions offering a much-needed new view of the disagreement.

## Find the First Domino

The same dynamics are at play in my decision cadence meetings. Those biweekly gatherings involve all my top managers coming together to solve one or two of the big issues holding our department or the entire organization back—and everyone knows I expect them to speak up.

For these meetings, the rules are a little stricter. Everyone has to do the pre-read before showing up, and if anyone has an opinion, they have to voice it in the meeting itself. I won't tolerate whispering after the fact about how they always knew some initiative would fail.

In the meeting, though, I encourage contrary opinions to be raised. If someone really believes we're pursuing a bad idea, I want to know. I want us to have that conversation.

I make it clear that there is a responsibility that comes with having a seat at the table, and this is true whether sitting at a business table or a dinner table. Everyone gathered for that discussion has a responsibility to speak up and share their concerns.

To make sure we use this time well, I also focus us on what I call "the first domino." When dealing with big, complex problems, it's easy to get bogged down either in the history of that problem or get lost going down any number of cul-de-sac side issues. To avoid this, we aim to make a decision on the first big domino that has to fall.

Line that one up correctly, and all the other dominos down the line—across all areas of the business—should follow suit. We don't need to get lost covering what happened twenty years ago or debate niche concerns. We have to attack the main problem and find a solution.

Each meeting should end with that domino ready to tip over. The only reason to delay a decision is if new information comes to light that we didn't know at the beginning of the discussion or if someone comes unprepared.

None of this guarantees that every decision will be the right one. But every decision will be a collective decision that we made using all available information. When we win, we win together. And when we fail, we do that together too.

It is also important to make clear that not every meeting results in a perfect alignment—with the topic under discussion resolved with a bow on it. Disagreements can linger. Individuals inevitably have blinders and deep biases that make it hard to come to a complete agreement. There are times when our meetings come to a stalemate, at which point, I set up one-on-one meetings to discuss the issues that continue to trouble some members.

In the end, we find a way, if not to consensus, then at least to mutual commitment on our next steps.

Again, as in business, so our personal life. Focusing on the actual issue at hand and putting a limit on how much history or side concerns are allowed into the discussion can be clarifying. Far too often, arguments in a relationship end up acting as a magnet, attracting all the half-swallowed slights and lingering hurt feelings that have built up over the years. By encouraging open conversation aimed at resolving the main topic under discussion, it's often possible to make real progress—so long as both parties are willing to follow those rules.

Like my business meetings, progress may not always look like complete agreement on the causes and solutions for that issue. But if you can avoid getting discouraged and keep making the effort, it can still look like a way forward.

## Eat and Make Up

The French have a stereotype for being rude, but in reality, they're just blunt. If they see you making a mistake, they'll point it out. If they think you're being inconsiderate, they won't ignore it; they'll call you out on it. They will do this in public as easily as they'll do it in private. This isn't meant to cause emotional harm so much as to air the truth and resolve the issue.

Ultimately, this kind of behavior is within all of our power. While it takes a bit of practice and emotional courage, anyone can learn how to debate ideas directly. We can all find it within ourselves to be forthright in our criticism. And we can all learn how to take feedback in the right spirit, absorb it, and move past hurt feelings.

But all of this has to start with leadership. We set the tone for our teams. If we encourage feedback and take criticism well, our people will be more willing to speak up and accept pushback from others. If, on the other hand, we're prickly every time someone objects to one of our ideas or we blame others when an initiative goes wrong, we can expect everyone to learn that the only things we accept are silence or praise.

We have to live the values of open conversation ourselves. It's relatively easy for a boss to give straightforward criticism to someone on their team, but we have to be willing to hear that criticism ourselves and to speak up to those above us in the hierarchy as well. If we see something wrong with a proposal before the executive committee and don't say anything, it is to the detriment of the whole company. We're in that position so we can say these things, not to be quiet.

I always end meetings by thanking everyone for helping all of us to understand the problem better. This reframes disagreements as being in service of the ultimate goal we all believe in. It reminds us all that we're on the same team.

At the same time, we have to create space for reconciliation after a tough conversation. A French boardroom may get noisy with contentious opinions about a key business priority, but afterward, there's always an effort to recenter relationships by talking about less intense topics. Often, as you might expect at this point, such reconciliation is done over a good meal.

A hearty meal heals a lot of hurt feelings, especially when paired with jovial conversation. If everyone engages in discussion with the company's—or, on a personal level, the relationship's—best interests at heart, a friendly chat while breaking bread is often just the trick to get everything back on track.

## *La Vie Française in America*

Three ways to start living the French lifestyle today

1. Create your own decision cadence. Pick your executive team or your family team and set aside time once or twice a month to discuss difficult topics—whether that be ERP selection or vacation destinations. Designate one person who will lead the discussion and send out a summary. Keep the conversation time bound. If you come to a decision quickly, people get that extra time back. The key is scheduling this time out.
2. Reduce the negative tension in your life. In your journal, do a monthly intake. Give yourself a checkmark if you had a negative thought about someone and didn't voice it. For instance, if you thought, "I sacrificed my job to raise these kids" but didn't state it, give yourself a check. If you did say it—but only in an argument—give yourself an "X" instead. At the end of the month, count your checks and Xs. Your aim is to reduce the number of both each month by sharing your thoughts in a positive way that helps move your relationships forward. To restate that again, the focus is on moving forward, not relitigating the past.
3. Admit you were wrong publicly. This may be due to an error or new information. When I publicly admitted that I had come in with one opinion and a decision cadence meeting had changed my mind, I noticed people became far more vocal and open minded. Show you are human and can be wrong, and people will respond.

# CHAPTER 9

## Mastering Moderation

Our apartment in Paris was almost regal in its beauty. It was on the third floor of one of those iconic Haussmannian buildings that you picture when you close your eyes and think of Paris. Stained glass windows lined the walls of the entryway, providing a patchwork of colorful light to guide us up the spiral staircase to our home. From our living room window, we had a straight view of the Eiffel Tower. Nothing could be more quintessentially Parisian than that.

But it was also quintessentially Parisian in its size. The total square footage of our apartment was only about a thousand square feet. Some of you have more closet space than that in your homes. Americans and Canadians are often shocked when I reveal that fact. *How could you live in such a tiny space, let alone cram a family of four in? Was there even room to breathe?*

Amazingly, not only did it not feel cramped, but it felt spacious. We had high ceilings and big windows. We even opened up a wall to give ourselves a bit of an open-concept living area. But most importantly of all, we knew how to use our space—and we knew how to choose how we filled it.

Living in small quarters teaches you to examine everything you own. Everything that has a place has to have a purpose. Every item of clothing should be worn regularly. Every plate should be used. There are no extra rooms that no one visits, no extra tables no one sits at, and no extra parking spaces with an extra car that no one drives regularly.

Instead, every item is the size and quality needed for long-term comfort and enjoyment. The fridges are smaller, but that allows you to buy more fresh food. The dishwashers are smaller, so you buy fewer, nicer dishes. You might not be able to fit a king-size bed into your bedroom, but a queen-size allows you to stay closer to your partner. Besides, in a smaller room, a queen really feels like a king anyway.

Everything becomes an exercise in moderation and sophistication. Our coatrack could only hold three jackets at a time, so each of us had one for each season that we found stylish and comfortable. The off-season jackets and coats were kept in a storage unit. We only had room for eight pairs of shoes in our closet in the entryway, just enough for Fayyaz and I to have a couple for work and a couple for leisure, with the kids having a pair or two each.

We never felt this small space limited us in making it our own or making it feel comfortable. When we moved in, the apartment had two bedrooms, but we were able to make it into three so each of our kids had their own space. When we opened up the wall of the living room and dining room, we added a charming arch to leave a sense of separate space.

It was everything we needed in a home, all in a thousand square feet. In a way, it felt more homey because of its size and the constraints that size put upon us. It's amazing how comfortable you can feel when forced to make more moderate, considered choices.

This lesson in thoughtful minimalism wasn't just about making the most of a smaller space—it revealed a fundamental difference between European and American approaches to possessions and consumption. I discovered just how stark this contrast was when I returned to America.

## More Is Less

When I moved back to America, I hired movers to help me settle into my new home. What I remember most from that day is the look of confusion sprawled across all their faces after they'd carried in the last of my furniture, dishes, books, and clothing.

"Is that it?" they asked. "Where's all the rest of it?"

The confusion was understandable. By American standards, I had far too little *stuff.* As a woman, this was particularly apparent in my wardrobe. Every item of clothing I owned barely took up a quarter of my closet. This wasn't because I'd left everything behind in France or couldn't afford more *things* to fill my house. I'd simply come from a culture that prioritized quality over quantity.

Over here, we tend to reverse that and place quantity above all else. America, and much of the modern world in general, has a clear preference to always go for more and bigger at every opportunity. Our portion sizes are huge on this side of the Atlantic. So are our cars and our homes. But this obsession with size has many real downsides. Most importantly, such overconsumption affects our health. About

40 percent of Americans are obese.[67] This condition increases the likelihood of any number of health issues, from diabetes to stroke and osteoarthritis.[68] The ultimate result of all this risk is that obesity can take up to fourteen years off someone's life.[69]

Put simply, our culture encourages us to take too many calories in without providing much opportunity to work them all off each day.[70] A similar overindulgence exists in our relationship with alcohol. Look at many Western cultures, and you'll see an outright celebration of excess in this area. Whether it's college partying in America or the central place the pub holds in British culture, we not only excuse drinking, we often encourage it. And I don't think I need to belabor how unhealthy that choice is.[71]

And those huge cars and trucks of ours also increase risk, leading to more road fatalities.[72]

Everywhere you look, you see this more and bigger philosophy at work—and it often makes it harder to get what we actually need. I recently went to HomeGoods with my daughter, Aliya. It was August,

---

67 "Overweight and Obesity Statistics," *National Institute of Diabetes and Digestive and Kidney Diseases*, September 2021, https://www.niddk.nih.gov/health-information/health-statistics/overweight-obesity.

68 "Health Risks of Overweight and Obesity," *National Institute of Diabetes and Digestive and Kidney Diseases*, May 2023, https://www.niddk.nih.gov/health-information/weight-management/adult-overweight-obesity/health-risks.

69 Brooke Worthing, "Extreme Obesity Shaves Years off Life Expectancy," *National Institutes of Health Intramural Research Program*, January 23, 2020, https://irp.nih.gov/blog/post/2020/01/extreme-obesity-shaves-years-off-life-expectancy.

70 "Overweight and Obesity Causes and Risk Factors," *National Heart, Lung, and Blood Institute*, March 24, 2022, https://www.nhlbi.nih.gov/health/overweight-and-obesity/causes.

71 "The Risks of Drinking Too Much," *National Health Service*, October 24, 2022, https://www.nhs.uk/live-well/alcohol-advice/the-risks-of-drinking-too-much/.

72 "Vehicles With Higher, More Vertical Front Ends Pose Greater Risk to Pedestrians," *The Insurance Institute for Highway Safety*, November 14, 2023, https://www.iihs.org/news/detail/vehicles-with-higher-more-vertical-front-ends-pose-greater-risk-to-pedestrians.

and she was shopping for some things to put in her college apartment. Despite the fact it was the time of year when students across the country move into dorms and apartments, most of the store's floor space was filled with Halloween items—a holiday that was still more than two months away.

Stores such as HomeGoods fill their aisles with Halloween and Christmas stuff because Americans have become holiday shopping hoarders. At this point, it isn't enough to put up a couple strings of lights or carve a jack-o'-lantern; we're supposed to refit our entire homes every October and December—and there's even pressure to do the same for Thanksgiving, Valentine's Day, St. Patrick's Day, and Fourth of July.

Keeping up with such quantity over quality is costly. Not only do we spend more than we need on things that don't really improve our lives, but we often end up buying bigger and bigger homes to have space for all that stuff. This can lead to unnecessary financial stress. It is also a huge threat to our environment.[73]

In business, this same impulse convinces leaders to waste money on expensive company cars, large office spaces in expensive districts, unnecessary corporate jets, and more—all of which put more financial pressure on an organization than is necessary. These expenses can hold back growth and leave a company at greater risk during a downturn.

It's a lot of cost and a lot of risk, all to finance more than we actually need.

## Moderating Risk

Luckily, there's a better philosophy available—the antithesis of excess and overconsumption—moderation. Moderation not only improves

73 Eden Barletta, "The Hidden Costs of Overconsumption," *Climable*, November 26, 2024, https://climable.org/blog/2024/11/20/overconsumption.

physical health outcomes; it also has psychological benefits, such as increasing self-control, improving decision-making, and providing us with a greater sense of overall life satisfaction.[74] It's a quality that helps balance budgets and maintain quality of life. In other words, this is not a philosophy about living with *less*; it's about finding a smarter, healthier way to enjoy life more fully.

We can see the benefits of moderation very clearly when we consider how the French approach their wardrobe. Though France is known as the fashion capital of the world, that doesn't mean they constantly buy new outfits. The culture, in fact, is distinctly anti-fast fashion. Instead, the aim is to buy fewer things, each of which is high in quality and durability. Walk down any boulevard in Paris, and you'll notice that almost every woman has a Chanel bag—or a similarly upmarket equivalent. It isn't that French women are so much richer than us, nor that they scrimp and save to afford such high-end items; they simply buy fewer, nicer things—things they intend to use regularly and for years to come.

There are many virtues to such an approach. In the first place, it's ultimately cheaper. Instead of buying ten bags over the next decade, they buy one once and use it for a lifetime, even passing it on to the next generation. It only takes a few years for that investment to save them money. And while they have more money in their pocket, they get to look more chic.

A great book on this is *Lessons from Madame Chic* by Jennifer L. Scott. In it, Scott details the discoveries she made living in Paris, among them how to be fashionable and eat well while buying and using less. Its central insight will be familiar to all of us at this point: French chic is possible for all of us if we embrace their more-is-less philosophy.

---

74 Carlin Flora, "Moderation Is the Key to Life," *Psychology Today*, July 4, 2017, https://www.psychologytoday.com/us/articles/201707/moderation-is-the-key-life.

In France, there's no need to go out every cold season to spend hundreds on new boots, because you bought a high-quality pair four years ago. At most, you might need a quick, cheap stop at your local shoe repair shop. As the proprietor there will tell you, good leather actually improves over time.

These savings are all the more impressive when you consider how many of our clothing purchases we literally never wear. One study of eighteen thousand heads of households across twenty countries found that almost everywhere in the world, people overestimate how much of their wardrobe they wear. Americans were particularly bad at this. They assumed they wore 57 percent of their wardrobe each year. In reality, they only wore 18 percent.[75]

Having fewer things hanging in your closet also makes dressing less stressful. Instead of spending hours deliberating over what to wear while searching through hundreds of shirts, skirts, dresses, and pants, having a smaller closet with nicer items that suit your style means everything naturally goes well together. This approach actually decreases stress and increases the joy people feel in fashion.[76]

It's no coincidence that many CEOs have taken Steve Jobs's cue and simplified their own closets. Jobs was weary of developing "decision fatigue," a state of exhaustion that comes from our need to make so many decisions in modern life.[77] Simplifying his wardrobe

---

75 Marjorie van Elven, "People Do Not Wear at Least 50 Percent of Their Wardrobes, Says Study," *FashionUnited*, August 16, 2018, https://fashionunited.uk/news/fashion/people-do-not-wear-at-least-50-percent-of-their-wardrobes-according-to-study/2018081638356.

76 Aurore Bardey et al., "Finding Yourself in Your Wardrobe: An Exploratory Study of Lived Experiences With a Capsule Wardrobe," *International Journal of Market Research* 64, no. 1 (February 16, 2021): 113–131, https://doi.org/10.1177/1470785321993743.

77 Sara Berg, "What Doctors Wish Patients Knew About Decision Fatigue," *American Medical Association*, November 19, 2021, https://www.ama-assn.org/delivering-care/public-health/what-doctors-wish-patients-knew-about-decision-fatigue.

meant that was one area of decision-making he didn't have to focus on anymore—allowing him to use that brain energy elsewhere.

It also saved him time. The time spent choosing outfits doesn't just waste brain energy; it wastes your time. The thirty minutes it takes to choose between blouses is thirty minutes you could have enjoyed reading ahead of dinner or an extra thirty minutes you could have spent chatting with a friend. Our habits of overconsumption often consume a lot of our time.

Consider how much time you've wasted going shopping for clothing without buying anything. For many in America and Canada, that's multiple hours each month. In France, you only enter a shop when you already have an idea of what you need to buy. That means you don't waste time or money on what you don't need.

This approach to wardrobe even helps with gift shopping. Instead of everyone taking their $20 and buying small items that won't get used, a smaller wardrobe means everyone knows your tastes and what you're lacking. They can then pool their money to get one really nice item that you'll use for years.

Moderation generally offers a better way to spend our money and time. In chapter 5, I spoke of a friend of mine from Pitney Bowes who bought a house early in his career. He found a place he loved that he could afford at that time. He's now paid it off in full and lives without the financial concerns of a mortgage. Spending less on clothing, jewelry, food, alcohol, cars, and homes, we'd have so much left over to enjoy ourselves with. We'd live with less debt and financial pressure.

A smaller house means less time spent cleaning it. A smaller yard requires less time mowing. A smaller car takes less gas and comes with a smaller car payment. Just because you *can* afford these things doesn't mean they're better for you.

Instead of renting a storage unit or buying a shed for all the extra stuff you had, imagine living with only what comfortably fits in your home.

This isn't just a personal philosophy either. Moderation offers a counter to the philosophy of excess that has infected many companies. In *The Outsiders*, William N. Thorndike Jr. details what truly makes a great CEO. Many executives assume that a great CEO looks like Jack Welch, the former leader of General Electric (GE). It's not that this is entirely wrong, but Thorndike shows that all Welch did was run a little ahead of a really strong bull market. Over his twenty years in charge, GE saw about 20 percent average annual growth. But the S&P 500 went up 14 percent average annual growth in that same time. So, Welch really only did 6 percent better than the rest of the market—a great accomplishment, but nothing extraordinary.

On the other hand, one of the CEOs whom Thorndike profiles, Henry Singleton, wildly outperformed the S&P 500 over a period that included much more bearish markets. One of Singleton's secrets was moderation. Instead of falling into the trap of spending more on perks such as first-class flights and fancy company cars—IBM once invested in purchasing real Picassos—companies buy these extravagant purchases and often overpay for them because they can. Instead of buying value, they look to prove their worth through their excess.

Singleton, and the others whom Thorndike profiles in the book, did the opposite. They maintained scrutiny around costs. They only hired when operations became consistently stretched. The SaaS company Constellation exemplifies this ethos as well. It's an $8 billion company, but it has $2 billion in cash in 2024. This gives it a disproportionate advantage when interest rates are high, and demand becomes low, allowing it to acquire fairly priced companies without borrowing. Instead of the sugar rush from venture capital funding, it has a more sustainable growth model, building on its fundamentals. That leaves it less susceptible to collapse.

## A Balancing Act

If moderation were always easy, we'd see more of it. Most of us are aware that at least some forms of moderation are valuable, but it can be hard to create circumstances where that's always our default choice.

The easiest way to begin shifting your mindset on moderation is perhaps not the most obvious: a book about your health. In *French Women Don't Get Fat*, Mireille Guiliano offers a lot of tips on maintaining a healthy weight. But at the center of the book is the French perspective on keeping things balanced. French women weigh themselves all the time. They know their preferred weight. So, if they've gained a pound or lost a pound, they can make adjustments to get back to that number.

It's easier to lose or gain a pound than to lose or gain ten or twenty pounds after a long period of neglect. The key here isn't obsession; it's actually the opposite. These women set a baseline and moderate their behavior around it.

This allows us to be thoughtful about our choices and what we put in our bodies. We can decide when we want to cheat and how we're going to pay for it. No one is saying you can never eat a piece of cake, but nothing you put in your body is free. It all comes at a cost. You can eat a pain au chocolat, but if you do, your equilibrium tells you that you'll need to either work out for an hour, eat a lighter dinner, or accept a higher number on the scale as a consequence. Any of those options are OK, but you should recognize that you are making that choice each time.

A little excess on occasion is great. It's fun. But we should put limits on how often and how much we exceed our equilibrium—and focus on enjoying the excesses we really care about. The Glucose Goddess, Jessie Inchauspé, has pointed out that the body doesn't care what form of sugar you take in—it's all sugar—so choose the form you love most.[78] If you love chocolate mousse, make that your indulgence. Find ways to fit that into your equilibrium. You aren't doing yourself any extra good by denying yourself that treat while still drinking orange juice every morning.

We can bring this perspective to every area of our lives. Instead of buying a new shirt every time you go out, you can set a baseline for the number you need and stick to it. If you have ten shirts, don't buy any more new ones until you get rid of one of the old ones. Three new skirts? You need to donate three already in your closet.

To decide which skirts make the cut, you can use the KonMari Method. Named after Marie Kondo, this is a thoughtful method for considering what items in your life you really cherish and which you can let go of.[79]

This equilibrium forces us to be more thoughtful about what we do invest in. If it's clothes, setting limits allows us to choose higher-quality, longer-lasting items that will remain fashionable for years to come. Instead of wasting money on a new jacket every year or two, spend that money all at once on a really great one you'll keep for a decade.

We can do the same with makeup. A friend of mine has thirty colors of lipstick. I have two. Half of those colors will go bad before they get used up. I use one stick up and buy another. That simplicity requires that I find the color that I find most flattering for myself, and then I stick with that. Quality over quantity.

---

78 Jessie Inchauspé, "Glucose Goddess: The 10 Glucose Hacks!" posted September 19, 2024, by The Diary Of A CEO, YouTube, 100 min., 28 sec., https://www.youtube.com/watch?v=3esF-pNAM9c.

79 Marie Kondo, "What Is the KonMari Method™?" *KonMari.com*, https://konmari.com/about-the-konmari-method/.

Focusing on equilibrium also helps us see where we are being wasteful—where we're allowing excess to become our standard. This gets to the heart of the American home-buying strategy I've touched on above. Most Americans justify buying excess space by focusing on the exceptions. A family with two kids only needs three bedrooms to be comfortable. But Americans often buy *five* bedrooms just for those rare occasions when relatives come to visit. In France, people are satisfied with three bedrooms and just accept that they'll have to find somewhere to place their parents when they do come. It's not the end of the world if kids have to share a room for a week or if someone has to sleep in the living room for a few nights.

This is true of dining rooms that rarely get used, big basements that almost no one steps foot in, and enormous kitchens for families that rarely cook. All of these extras add more cost and financial pressure with little benefit. And once we have all that space, we feel we have to fill it with something—so once again, we're out buying more than we need.

It's far better to spend a little more time considering the space you actually need before signing your name on that next mortgage. Get a home that fits your everyday needs and find ways to adapt that space when you need to. If you buy what you can actually afford, with the space you actually need, and you stay there, you'll be in a far better financial position without really sacrificing much at all.

## Simplify, Simplify, Simplify

While finding balance and maintaining equilibrium are essential first steps, achieving true moderation often requires us to go further—to actively simplify our lives and our operations. This is true whether we're managing a household or running a major corporation.

Complexity is often what kills companies. Bloated, complex operations are more than confusing; they're expensive, and they can lead to any number of errors. Simplicity, though, is hard to maintain. You may start out with a simple product and a simple process, but over time, exceptions tend to creep into the works, adding ever more complexity to processes and organization. It's easy to give in to every request from every client. If you're worried about losing talent in the organization, it's easy to green-light a few company cars. But once you make an exception, you have to be willing to do it again.

Over time, this complexity becomes standard. Company cars go to everyone at a certain level, regardless of their overall need or value to the organization. Custom projects are offered to every client, whether they bring in significant revenue or not. Exceptions become the rule, clogging up every process.

The cure for this is increased simplicity, and to achieve that, you have to establish priorities. A business has to know what numbers matter, what goals matter, and what clients matter most. By attending to those priorities, it's easier to see where complexity is holding the organization back.

On a personal level, priorities can play just as important a role. *18 Minutes* by Peter Bregman helped me come up with my own list of priorities that I try to live by for an entire year. Every year, I pick three personal and two work priorities at a time. I set these at the end of each year, and I check in on them every week. Every Sunday, late in the afternoon, I look over the previous week's agenda to see if I've attended to all my priorities. By analyzing the data of my life, I see if I spent enough time on what really matters. If not, where did my time go, and how can I rebalance it?

Using this simple method, I went from spending about 10 percent of my time on my priorities to 80 percent. This led to real, tangible results in my life. It's no coincidence that I only really started getting promoted at a much more rapid rate after I implemented this priority system.

Obviously, there are weeks when I fall short. I get sick, or there's a major project I have to complete. But overall, like those French women who don't get fat, I'm able to rebalance and refocus afterward.

With those explicit priorities, I avoid pushing off what really matters. I've had three CEOs in the last year. It would be the easiest thing in the world to say it's not the right time to focus on exercise or reading more. If you've got young kids, a new romantic relationship, or a new job, it never feels like the right time to attend to yourself.

But the truth is, there's always something demanding your attention. By laying your priorities out and reviewing your week to make sure you're putting time into them, you keep progressing, even when life is full of responsibilities.

## Reduce Temptation

One final way to achieve moderation and balance is to simply reduce the risk of temptation. I know how fun it is to hang out in shopping malls and go to nice clothing stores, but when you do, it's always so tempting to buy just one cute blouse or one pair of shoes that seems to really suit you. To avoid the extra clutter, you should just stop going.

Or find a workaround. I like to go window shopping after stores are closed. That way, I can see what's on display without the risk of an impulse purchase. The same is true for our food. There's an old rule to avoid going to the grocery store hungry, and it's a good one. How often have you gone to Costco for some pasta and pesto, only to walk out with $300 of groceries? Shop for food online—ideally after a nice meal—so you can make more considered choices. If you order fresh food every few days and just stop by to pick it up, you reduce excess purchases that cost more, take up space, and usually include a number of unhealthy choices.

In truth, whether it's finding your equilibrium, setting priorities, or avoiding temptation, the key to moderation is increasing how much thought you put into your choices. Do you really need another new nail polish? What about that second home? Those feel like very different types of decisions, but we arrive at the right choice the same way: by really thinking through what we want and what we need.

I know a couple—Jessica and Ryan—who were considering buying a second property—a beach home in an area they always enjoyed visiting. Jessica, in particular, was eager to make the purchase. She didn't want the place for an investment. Any use of the property for a rental was incidental to her; she just wanted a vacation home she always knew was there when she felt like visiting.

When they sat down to think about it, though, the money really didn't make sense. Technically, they could afford it, but as Ryan pointed out, they were basically throwing away an entire house's worth of money. They would be paying an entire mortgage—plus electricity, gas, insurance, and property tax—for a place they would only occasionally visit. This was not a location they could get to every weekend. Most of the time, it would just sit there. Besides the money, the investment wasn't worth the cost in their peace of mind.

How many trips would it take to justify buying that second house? Just because they *could* do it didn't mean it was the right call. It would be far better, they realized, to just rent a house every time they went to that location. That would allow them to travel to other places and to save more toward their retirement.

It was a big, excessive purchase—one they were better off avoiding.

## Invest Instead of Excess

So, if you don't buy that extra house, what exactly should you do with your resources? If you shrink down your wardrobe and save instead of buying another massive vehicle, what do you do with the money sitting in your account?

The answer to that will be different for each person, but there are a few things to consider. I've mentioned before my colleague who bought his financial freedom by focusing on saving enough so he doesn't have to work if he doesn't want to. He doesn't have to rely on Social Security. He's set for life at a level he finds comfortable. It's hard to overestimate the value of that kind of position. The younger you can achieve it, the better.

Beyond that, we can reframe the entire concept of consumption. The thing you purchase instead of those excesses is not necessarily more *stuff*; it's your health and time. You can have more money for those dream vacations you've always wanted to take. Instead of scrimping to cover plane tickets and staying wherever you can afford, bump up to business class and stay in the city center in Paris or Rome for a trip that really matters.

You can have more energy because you're eating better—and will likely live longer. You can have more time on weekends because you don't have to spend as long maintaining that enormous house. That's time to spend with your spouse, your kids, and your friends. It's time you can spend building those relationships with neighbors and really getting involved in your community.

Isn't that worth the price of having the biggest house in the neighborhood?

Whatever it is, you can take those resources you gain from cutting the excess and invest them in the things that really matter to you. I have this beautiful purse I purchased years ago. It was really expensive, but I knew I was going to use it regularly for a long time. It's still in great condition. These days, I've been thinking about how nice it will be to hand it down to my daughter, Aliya.

I'm sure she'll get use out of it for many years to come—and I'm sure it'll mean more than receiving yet another purse that she'll use for a few years and then throw out. To me, that's a gift worth cutting back for.

## *La Vie Française in America*

Three ways to start living the French lifestyle today

1. Depending on the area of your life you want to work on first, read one of the following:

    a. French Women Don't Get Fat

    b. The Life-Changing Magic of Tidying Up

    c. Lessons from Madame Chic

2. Practice the "zero-sum" or "negative-sum" game: If you add something to your wardrobe, makeup, toys, etc., the same amount or more should come out. You can donate these items or give them to a friend or a sibling, but they have to leave your house.
3. Use *18 Minutes* by Peter Bregman to set your main priorities for the year.

# CHAPTER 10

## Cultivating Contentment

When I think of the perfect moment, I have this one photo in mind. I call it *Contentment*. The image shows a tree in the front yard of our house outside Chantilly, with a bicycle leaning against it. White flowers had recently blossomed and fallen from its branches, and the petals are still scattered across the green grass like summer snow. The sky is clear and sunny. It's a simple portrait of a warm, pleasant day, but what makes it so special to me is what it doesn't show.

I took that picture inside our home, through the open French doors that led from the yard into our living room where I worked. On a pleasant May day like that, I always liked to leave those doors open so I could smell the fresh scent of jasmine and lily wafting in from the garden. From the door, I could also hear my kids on the street as they noisily made their way home after school. What would start as a distant murmur would turn into a din once I heard the gate swing open and clatter shut, announcing their arrival.

On that particular day, my kids had just come home. They smelled of the fresh pain au chocolat they'd picked up on the way home, which they'd been so eager to enjoy that they'd finished it before even reaching the house. As they got settled, they tried to stifle their laughter long enough to tell me all about their day—the little adventures they'd encountered over the last eight hours at school.

The stories weren't that interesting or important; what really mattered in that moment was how eager they were to tell me. As I looked out the window at our yard, I remember breathing deeply and thinking, *Don't forget this. This is what life is supposed to be like.* I felt blessed that I was home to share this moment with them. I was there to hear their stories.

For a brief moment, I felt that time wasn't working against me. And so, I immortalized it in a photo, an image I could turn to and remind myself what really matters—what really brings me joy.

## The Power of Contentment

I called that photo *Contentment* on purpose, even though most would probably have chosen the word we often reach for in such moments: *happiness.* Undeniably, I was happy that afternoon, but I've come to prefer the former term. The difference between the two is important. Happiness gets all the press, but it's an inconsistent emotion. By its nature, it's up and down. You're high, and then you're low. No one is happy all the time; it's too intense an emotion to maintain.

Contentment is the opposite. It's steady, a form of happiness watered down by a general satisfaction about life. It removes both the peaks and the valleys of happiness, allowing for a consistent, positive, and peaceful emotional state.

So often, we mix these two emotions up. The former chief business officer at Google, Mo Gawdat, wrote an entire book called *Solve for Happy*, which is really about his journey to contentment, not happiness.

That said, the advice he shares in that book is excellent. The roots of his story are tragic, charting Gawdat's journey to happiness after the death of his son. A mathematician, he spent years developing an equation for happiness—an algorithm of contentment. At its heart, Gawdat's math is meant to equal a kind of freedom that comes from a lack of expectation. Is rain happy or sad? It's neither—unless you were planning for sunshine or hoping for the end of a drought. If we remove those expectations, we can remain in a steady state of contentment, no matter what happens.

It's true that steadiness and contentment aren't known for being exciting emotions. The reason we reach for happiness instead is that it feels livelier and more intense. And Americans are all about that. Over on this side of the Atlantic, we love to look for constant change and improvement—to disrupt, to "move fast and break things." With that mentality, there's no time to slow down and appreciate what's going right.

But this focus on growth and finding something bigger and newer all the time can cause some real problems. As we saw in the last chapter, it leads to overconsumption. It also causes a lot of stress—and that stress may be killing us.[80] Even putting our health aside, though, a perspective focused solely on our highest highs and more ebullient

80 Robert J. Samuelson, "Is the American Dream Killing Us?" *The Washington Post*, April 2, 2017, https://www.washingtonpost.com/opinions/is-the-american-dream-killing-us/2017/04/02/2827f4b6-1633-11e7-9e4f-09aa75d3ec57_story.html.

joys robs us of the positive emotions we should be feeling from more everyday accomplishments and triumphs. When we're always looking for the next challenge, the next promotion, the next raise, we're never living in the moment and enjoying what we have.

In France, there's much more focus on joie de vivre—an embrace of contentment across life, whether in moments of success or failure, joy or sorrow. This emotionally balanced perspective is as healthy as the hunt for a bigger, better hit of jubilation is unhealthy. Contentment may allow us to step off the hedonistic treadmill that keeps us constantly adjusting to every new level of success and, therefore, being as dissatisfied as ever.[81] It can make us more resourceful, lower our blood pressure, and allow us to sleep better.[82]

Contentment and its cousin, fulfillment, also make workers more engaged, motivated, and committed to their jobs. This can result in increased productivity, better customer service, and a more positive work environment for everyone.[83] And perhaps it goes without saying, but a contented person is just easier to get along with, which means relationships improve with more contentment.[84]

Put another way, our ambitions, if left unchecked, can make us more miserable no matter how much we succeed. Our quest for a particular position or for perfect happiness has no end, and the journey can be a disappointing one. Fortunately, there's a far clearer path to contentment.

---

81 Jessica Koehler, "The Quiet Power of Contentment," *Psychology Today*, November 22, 2023, https://www.psychologytoday.com/us/blog/beyond-school-walls/202311/the-quiet-power-of-contentment.

82 "How Happiness Impacts Health," *Northwestern Medicine*, https://www.nm.org/healthbeat/healthy-tips/how-happiness-impacts-health.

83 Remez Sasson, "Strategies for Unlocking the Incredible Power of Contentment," *Success Consciousness*, https://www.successconsciousness.com/blog/happiness-fun/the-power-of-contentment/.

84 Ibid.

# The Emotion of Acceptance and Adjustment

Contentment is not a fast-paced emotion. It's more a lazy river than white water rapids. But one of its great benefits is that it allows you the space to accept the unexpected and adjust to changes in your reality.

The challenge of maintaining contentment amid life's unexpected turns reminds me of those strategy games on your phone—you know, the kind where you build objects one piece at a time? They're great time wasters and fun little brain teasers you can play through while waiting to see the doctor or get a table for dinner. The most frustrating thing about those games, though, is when you purposely set a piece aside to use later, only for something unexpected to happen in the game. Suddenly, that piece won't fit, or worse, holding onto it means you lose the game.

That's how life can be sometimes. No matter how carefully and thoroughly you plan, the unexpected can always derail you. You can research an investment for a year, chart a company's progress, and research every member of its executive team, but a recession or a corporate scandal can still cost you every dollar you put in.

You can carefully organize your time for your whole week and get every responsibility completed by Saturday night so you'll have a completely free Sunday. But you can't keep one of your kids from getting the flu or a friend calling and needing some emergency support.

I've experienced this very thing recently. When I started writing this book, I did everything to set myself up for success. I was in a steady position where my obligations and time commitments were clear. I had a CEO I knew well, and I had a strong working relationship with him. I'd done the early work, put together notes and outlines, and budgeted the time to write and edit. I was all ready to reap the rewards of my careful planning and hard work.

Then, the company hit a rough patch. The CEO was exited, then the interim CEO was exited. The company decided to shut down one of its business units while we went through a top-to-bottom complete company overhaul.

We all know this can happen, but in such moments, the worst thing we can do is give into our natural impulses to dig in or dwell on how the world has wronged us. We can get so invested, so focused on our goal, and so tantalizingly close to achieving it that we lose all our ability to be flexible. We prepare for perfect, and when things go wrong, we moodily try to cling to the old plans. That stubbornness inevitably sets us up to fall short and disappoint our ambitions.

Contentment can offer a different way. Instead of trying to continue to push ahead when a tree falls right in the middle of the path we were following, we can meet the challenge with acceptance and resilience. We can adjust, compromise, and find another way through.

With a little equanimity, we can take a breath and reset our priorities. That's what I did with this book. The writing process didn't go as quickly as I'd hoped or planned. It wasn't as easy to find the hours to put these ideas down on paper. But accepting reality allowed me to build a new plan—one that allowed me to get the book done even while I put fires out every day in the office. It took me an extra six months, but as you can see, it did get done.

The acceptance we gain through contentment of our limited role in seeing our plans through can also provide us with the space we need to maneuver into a new path because it encourages us to slow down. We can't keep running at full speed as individuals or as companies. Speed puts pressure on every system. When unexpected issues come up, they're harder to fix because you can't turn easily at top speed.

Often, pivoting when facing the unexpected can take longer than we anticipate. Changing a company culture can take years, sometimes as long as a decade. When you discover you have issues with culture, you can't fix it at top speed. That's why European companies tend to move slower but have more robust and long-lasting outcomes.

We all know we have to expect the unexpected in life. People get sick. Economies go into recession. Companies hit difficult times. We want a clear plan in place for these moments, but that isn't enough. We also need to be moving at the pace of contentment so we have the space and the energy reserves to adjust when we have to.

## Keep Life Simple

I've talked a lot in this book about simplicity. Finding a home that fits your life instead of the biggest one on the block is a lesson in simplicity. Eating better meals while doing fewer things is a simpler way of eating. Putting the phone away during conversations, freeing up time on your Sundays, having straightforward conversations with neighbors—these are all lessons in simplifying life.

You may have heard the phrase, "Complexity is the enemy of execution." There's a lot of truth in that, but complexity is also the enemy of contentment. If you're always trying to do ten things at once—if you are permanently busy and distracted—it's almost impossible to simply be in the moment. How can you appreciate all that is right in your life when you have to jump from task to task without a break?

This is why our first step toward contentment has to be building balance and simplicity into every part of our lives. Much of this can be done using the tools we've already covered in this book.

To take this effort even further, though, I recommend that everyone engage in a regular *vide-grenier*. In France, once a year, the city comes by and picks up larger items off the curb for free. All the old furniture and heavy boxes of old stuff sitting in your home can finally get cleared away. Since almost everyone lives in apartments with limited space, this is a really big deal. Whether people have beds their kids have outgrown, old clothes that no longer fit, or a couch that's become too soft and lumpy, it can all go out on the street.

This requires everyone to engage in a bit of reflection. Ahead of the big day, they have to consider what items they're ready to part with and which ones they feel they want to hold onto for at least another year. Are they really ready to get rid of that set of dishes and buy a new one, or are they OK eating on the old plates a little longer? Do they want to spend money on a new TV stand, or will the old one do until next spring?

As a side note, while all these items are put out for trash, at least half are actually taken away by other French people. It's quite common to see trucks from local upholsterers driving around the streets ahead of the big pickup, finding items they can fix up and resell. One person's lumpy couch is another person's new relaxing sofa.

Regardless, there's value in doing this kind of spring cleaning in your own life. Mentally and physically—in your home, your body, and your mind—do an inventory. Do you need every item in your house right now? What about every habit you've developed? Are you really enjoying your meals more because you're on your screen? Do you really get more from life going out every Friday?

Maybe, but it's worth asking the question and getting a clear answer. And you may find there are activities, obligations, and objects you can cut from your life to simplify it. Instead of cramming your days so full that there's no room for contentment, give yourself the space to live and find a little balance.

Ask yourself this: If an urgent thing came up, what is the first thing you'd *choose* to drop to make space for it? That word *choose* is key here. The question isn't about what you're most likely to drop; it's what you want to drop. If we don't make this choice before we need to, we're more likely to drop the things we really care about instead of the things we can most easily dispose of. We'll drop our exercise routines, our meal planning, and our time with the kids. Instead of losing what matters, put what doesn't out on the street corner—and enjoy all that extra space.

## Memento Mori

Contentment can be drawn from many sources, even the morbid. Frankly, the French think about death a lot. They talk about death in casual conversation. While in America this would be a faux pas, in France, it is an uncomfortable but important topic because it clarifies what we're doing and whether we're living well.

I had a neighbor in France who had a particular dish I really liked. Whenever I stopped by, I always complimented her on it. One day, she came over and just gave it to me.

"I can't take that," I said. "You love this dish."

"Look," she told me. "I'm eighty-two. I'm going to die eventually. I don't want my kids to have the burden of clearing away all my stuff. And they don't care about this thing. I would have wanted you to have it anyway, so now you can enjoy it while I'm alive."

Recognizing that we only have so much time makes it easier to see what matters and what doesn't. Captain Tom Moore—the one-hundred-year-old British man who became famous during the

COVID-19 pandemic for raising more than $40 million for health-care workers by walking around his garden—wrote a book afterward detailing his life.[85] In it, he mentioned how he did just as my neighbor had. In his eighties, he invited his kids over and asked them to take what they wanted. He knew he only had so much time left. In the end, he actually had almost twenty years, but he'd cleared away all the extras: He'd simplified his life for the remaining time he had.

When we look toward our end, some questions hit us with particular force. When considering how to invest my time and energy, I often ask myself, what will I regret *least* in the future? Will I regret turning down a promotion? Certainly, but I'd regret missing time with my kids more than I'd regret missing out on a job.

We owe it to ourselves to be clear about what's most important. As I discussed in the last chapter, prioritizing responsibilities and opportunities is always a challenge, particularly in the busy, hectic years of career growth and young children. Casting our eyes to the end can give some much-needed perspective. It allows us to focus on what is most important. For me, it's time: time with family, time with friends, time for myself. I also care about purpose. I want to do work that I feel matters. I want to give back to my community and interact with people. I want balance. I may not be able to attend to those priorities at every moment, but recognizing that time is a limited resource helps me refocus on how I'm spending it.

My *Contentment* photo depicts a particular day when I got it all right, but there were plenty of times when I didn't. Once, I was on a phone call when the kids got home. They ran up to me, eager to share some story or other from their day, only to be shushed by the

---

85 Captain Tom Moore, *Tomorrow Will Be a Good Day: My Autobiography* (Penguin Books Limited, 2020).

babysitter. They knew the rules. When Mommy is on the phone, you have to wait to speak.

Quietly, then, they went off to the living room, where they fervently told this story to the babysitter. When I showed up thirty minutes later, I asked what was so exciting, but it was too late. They weren't interested in sharing it a second time. I'd missed the moment.

Those lost experiences are inevitable in life. It's impossible to capture every single story that your kids will ever want to tell you. We have to work. We have to live our own lives. And focusing solely on your kids isn't good for them. But it's also easy to let those occasional missed moments become the standard.

Whenever I miss one, I think of the song "Cat's in the Cradle" by Harry Chapin, in which a father is too busy for his son all through the boy's childhood. When the father finally has time in his old age, it's too late. His son has become too busy for him, and he has no reason to prioritize the old man.

We all have those "Cat's in the Cradle" moments, but by casting an eye to the end of the song more often, we can make sure they happen rarely.

## Change Your Expectations

For ambitious, talented people, the qualities that help them excel are often the ones that make it harder to be content. If you expect a mansion with five cars, it's hard to be satisfied with three bedrooms and two cars. If you want to be a CEO living in Manhattan, an executive position in Colorado Springs probably feels like a letdown. If you expect to jet-set around the world, you won't find much contentment in a couple of wonderful two-week vacations a year.

So often, we want these things not for our own personal sense of contentment but for some form of social status. Do you want to live in New York City because you love the city or because it signifies success? Do you need the mansion because your family is really that big or because it suggests you really "made it"? Are you trying to become head of neuroscience at Johns Hopkins because you believe you can run that department better than anyone else or because it would impress your family and friends?

Contentment requires recognizing what we actually care about and focusing on fulfilling those needs, even if we have to change our expectations elsewhere. I know plenty of sellers who make more money than me, but I just don't care that much about having the biggest paycheck in the company. I love building teams and lifting people up. I love leading the way. So that's the direction I've taken in my career. So long as I'm doing that, I'm content.

Success doesn't have to mean climbing the ladder; it can be about finding the space where you belong—your métier. There is, undeniably, an income level where a promotion makes a difference for you and your family, but once you hit that point, another boost in your bank balance won't make much of a difference ultimately. Once you have enough to cover the home you want, the family you care for, and the necessary expenses of life with a little left over—does the next promotion really matter? Especially when you consider the cost in terms of your time and stress levels?

I have heard from so many people that they're doing their job for the kids. But if any of them actually asked their kids what they'd want for their parent's careers, I know what most would choose. They'd want whatever job allows their parent to be more contented, more active, more energized, and more present. That's better than all the possible toys they could get at Christmas.

In this way, contentment can become our yardstick for success. Instead of aiming for a particular object, aim for a sense of satisfaction with your place in the world.

Every now and again, I like to run a test every Sunday night. As I get ready for bed, I ask myself if I'm sad that the next day is a Monday. If I am, I know something is off. I'm not in the right position. I'm not striking the right life–work balance. Something needs to change.

If you ask yourself this often enough, and if you act on the results, I'm confident you'll find over time that you're less disappointed to begin a new week and more contented.

## The Good Life

As I reflect on all these elements of a well-lived life—the balance, the simplicity, the acceptance—I keep returning to that afternoon captured in *Contentment.* And I'm not the only one who remembers such moments so fondly. My kids also think of that time as a golden era for our family. My son, Qaahir, once told me it was when we were happiest as a family. He even wrote his essay for Cornell about it. Believe it or not, the subject of the paper was contentment as the meaning and purpose of life.

What made that period in our lives so special was the fact I had the time and the energy to focus on the things I truly feel are important. These were often small events—a story from the kids, a chance to play pretend in the afternoon, snuggling up to watch a movie—but these are the moments that make a contented, even joyful, life.

Many of the ideas in this book offer such moments of contentment—if we're willing to capture them. A Sunday spent in a museum, a really good meal spent with friends or colleagues, a great conversation with neighbors, a free afternoon with the spouse when the kids are being watched by the grandparents. None of those mean much in concrete terms, but in another sense, they really mean everything.

Even if you don't have all this in your life yet, part of contentment is recognizing the little things that are going right at the moment. Whenever I lose track of how good life is, I try to free up time on a weekend and do a level set. I take it easy and think about all the good things in my life right now.

On these level-set weekends, I essentially take a mini-staycation. I let my body clock wake me up. I go for a nice walk. On these walks, I stop and chat with the people I know. I pet the neighbor's dog when she's out. I get a good meal and make sure I enjoy every bite. If I pass our local bakery, Raphaël's, I stop and enjoy the smell. I look out for smiling children as they run around the playground. I help an elderly neighbor cross the street or carry her groceries. Or, sometimes, I just take a moment to have a conversation with a seemingly lonely soul.

I take a beat to just breathe and to live. Then I make sure I appreciate it all. At some point during the weekend, I write about all the good things in my life. My family is healthy and doing well overall. We are all still close and care deeply for one another.

When I take a moment like that, often I realize I really am living *la belle vie*. I've just been too busy and stressed to see it.

## *La Vie Française in America*

Three ways to start living the French lifestyle today

1. Pick your own vide-grenier day. Based on your work/family calendars, choose a date—mine is the third Sunday in May—to get rid of the old items taking up space in your home. A month ahead of the big day, work with your family to go through clothes, decorations, dishes, furniture, and anything else you plan on replacing. Make a list, schedule a donation or furniture removal service to come by on your chosen date, and get everything you no longer need out.
2. Find your contentment moment from the past. List out the things that made it special. Pick one to three tactical items you can do or change today to return to that state again. For instance, if that moment of contentment included playing with your kids outside, you can still recreate it by having a picnic with them when they're grown up. If the moment was quiet time doing research in a library while you were in college, recreate that with a really interesting book next to the fireplace or while you take a relaxing bath.
3. Read Hal Elrod's *The Miracle Morning* and Robin Sharma's *The 5AM Club* to get some new ideas on waking up early to build a contentment perspective. In particular, wake up thirty to sixty minutes earlier so you can do some self-care such as meditating, exercising, and writing in a gratitude journal. The benefits are worth the change in your sleep schedule.

# CONCLUSION

People come to me all the time at work and say things like, "Oh, you're so human," or "You're so down to Earth." What they mean by this is that I seem put together. I seem kind. I have time to focus on them and their individual journeys. I'm not always rushed, brusque, or focused solely on deadlines and data points. I recognize that emotions, trust, and change take time.

When I get a compliment like that, I always give the same response: "That's my French side." And it truly is—every aspect of how I approach work and life today has been shaped by my years in France. It's there that I learned how to live this way and present myself the way I do to others. In France, I learned to take the time I needed to relax and recover. It's where I learned to safeguard my weekends and make them count. The French taught me to savor my meals and make real connections while breaking bread. They showed me the value of outside interests and making my career my own.

I learned to leverage relationships and build communities. I learned how to have real conversations with people, the importance of balance and moderation, and the true value of contentment.

I hope I've convinced you as well that the French are onto something—that it's worth cultivating your own French side. Some of that cultivation can be done quickly, but I recognize that much of the advice I've shared requires time and a bit of work. Just as you don't change a company's culture overnight, it can take some time to find hobbies, build relationships in your community, and organize your time so you're getting rest and fulfillment outside the office.

At the same time, I know it's not possible to fully implement a French lifestyle in America or Canada. Believe me, I've tried. But I've also tried throughout this book to offer ways you can get as close as possible without having to fly across the Atlantic. Simply taking advantage of the opportunities and mindsets already available to you can get you pretty close to solving the Paris Paradox.

Another reason people say such things to me is because I make a point of telling people the *why* of what we're doing. Instead of being left trying to puzzle through why we're taking on a particular project or aiming for a particular goal, I explain it to them so they can be involved in the decision—and even offer new, better suggestions for how we can achieve it.

I want to do the same here. So, here's the *why* behind this book. There's a lot that is great about America and Canada. But I see people all around me who are stressed, stretched for time, exhausted, unhealthy, and unhappy. These are people who are successful overall by almost any standard, but they don't seem to be enjoying it much. I believe adding a little French wisdom to such people's lives can be a major corrective.

That said, there's every reason to believe you can absorb and live these values in North America. In this book, I've focused on what the French can teach us, but Canada and America are countries that lend themselves to people finding their own best way to live. In fact, I once asked my local French bakers, the owners of the fabulous Raphaël's, if they'd ever want to go back to France.

"No," they told me. "We love the US. We love how friendly people are. We love the entrepreneurial spirit and the way things are organized to help start new businesses. We love the clean streets and the way they pay people for their work."

In an environment like that, there's no reason we can't carve out more Sundays and get closer to our neighbors. The goal of this book isn't to convince people to become French. Rather, it's to incorporate the French principles and values that feel authentic and meaningful to you.

I've always said the ideal form of employment is working for an American company in France. It offers the best of both worlds. You get the efficiency and ambition of American business with the life–work balance of France. And I think that balance should be the aim of anyone reading this book. If the ideas I've laid out appeal to you, seek a way to create the hybrid structure in your own life, focusing on the ideas that would most improve your sense of contentment.

And whatever you do, don't stop learning and adding new ideas from France and elsewhere. If you visit France, make the effort to meet the people where they are. The old stereotype that French people are rude is mostly unfounded. They aren't rude; they're waiting for you to make an effort.

Back when I was at IBM, an executive vice president flew in from America to close a deal. When all the documents were signed, we all went to dinner together. He left the table after only forty-five minutes.

We hadn't even gotten to dessert! The French businesspeople were all shocked. They told me that if I hadn't been on the deal, they would have pulled out.

So often, this is how we approach other cultures, expecting them to bend to our standards, to share their perspective at our pace, with as little effort from us as possible. But if you try to speak a little French and show some genuine curiosity about their culture, you may be surprised how much the French will open up and share with you.

And you don't have to stop with the French. I'm sure there are just as many great pieces of advice for living to be found in China, Japan, India, or Iran. Old cultures have had the time to try out and refine many ideas, and the ones that stick, that most people in that area live by, often have some value to them.

If you let go of your preconceived notions of what the right way to live is, you may be surprised how much you can learn—and how far what you learn can take you. Ultimately, that's what I hope you take from the book. It's best to learn through living, not just from a book.

So go live the Paris Paradox. Try out a little life–work balance. And enjoy the *joie* it can bring to your *vie*.

# THE PARIS PARADOX

In the city where the clock slows down,
Life whispers softly, not with a frown.
Cobblestones echo with measured pace,
Each step a story, each moment grace.
Here, work bows humbly to life's demand,
Vacations sacred, leisure grand.
Not the rush, but the rhythm remains,
Building a life free of needless chains.
Peace of mind flows like the Seine,
Contentment found in the now and then.
A balance struck, a harmony true,
In quiet moments, the soul renews.
A café table, a spirited debate,
Passion in words, decisions await.
The collective voice, the harmony sought,
Better together, wisdom is wrought.

Streets so narrow, yet endlessly wide,
Where love and laughter comfortably reside.
Small spaces, optimized with care,
Beauty and function in a perfect pair.
From morning strolls to twilight's glow,
Pleasure in moments that gently flow.
A baguette's crunch, a painter's hue,
Everyday wonders felt anew.
Joie de vivre, the city's embrace,
A lesson in cherishing time and space.
Build things to last, with heart and hand,
A legacy rooted, a life well planned.
Oh Paris, paradox of delight,
You teach us to savor, to pause, to ignite.
In your essence, a truth profound:
The best of life is always around.

# ACKNOWLEDGMENTS, ET VOILÀ!

This book would not have been possible without the incredible people who supported me along the way.

First and foremost, to my brilliant and tireless publication team—Alison, Seth, Whitney, Elizabeth, Lindsey, Matthew, and the rest of the crew—merci infiniment for your patience, insight, and sheer dedication. I had not fully grasped the army it takes to bring a book to life, and I am endlessly grateful for your expertise.

To my dream team in the US—Colin, Gitika, Melanie, Ruchi, Beth, Chris, Dorene, Chetan, Greta, Marsha, Surya, and Carl—your friendship, stories, and unwavering belief in my ideas (even when they were half-baked) made this adventure all the more rewarding. Mille mercis for being my willing cobayes as I tested theories on you!

To my French inspirations—Silvano, Laurence, Angela, Didier, Hillary, and Laura—merci pour la magie française that infused this project with creativity, culture, and a certain *je ne sais quoi.*

A special *merci du fond du cœur* to Raphaël's for their countless croissants, coffee, and conversations—fueling both my mind and spirit through this journey.

To my family—Fayyaz, Qaahir, and Aliya—who embarked on this grand adventure with me, your love and support are my greatest treasures.

And finally, to you, cher lecteur, for giving this book a chance—merci mille fois!

After many late nights, an ocean of coffee, and a sprinkle of French inspiration—et voilà! This book is yours now. Bonne lecture et à bientôt!

# ABOUT THE AUTHOR

Shemin Nurmohamed spent nearly two decades living and working in France, where she discovered a profoundly different approach to balancing life and work. As a mother of two young children and an executive at IBM, she learned to embrace longer lunches, proper vacations, and the art of savoring life's moments—lessons that transformed both her career and her family life. Today, she serves as executive vice president and president of Sending Technology Solutions at Pitney Bowes, where she implements these French-inspired principles to build stronger, more connected teams.

Born in Tanzania and educated at Cornell University, Shemin brings a unique cross-cultural perspective to questions of work, family, and finding contentment in our busy modern lives. Her journey from a chemistry teacher in Paris to a global executive has given her firsthand experience in adapting French wisdom to the American workplace. When she's not leading corporate strategy or mentoring the next generation of leaders, Shemin can be found enjoying long

Sunday afternoons with her family, exploring local museums, or sharing croissants and conversation with neighbors at her favorite French bakery near her Connecticut home.

Drawing on her experiences living on both sides of the Atlantic, she is passionate about helping others find their own version of work–life balance—or, as she prefers to call it, life–work balance. She shares these insights regularly as a speaker at conferences across the US, Europe, and the Middle East. Shemin lives with her husband, Fayyaz, and their two children, who still count their years in France as some of their happiest memories as a family.